Mountain Biking
Durango

JOHN PEEL

FALCON® Helena, Montana

ᴀFALCONGUIDE®

Falcon® Publishing is continually expanding its list of recreational guidebooks. All books include detailed descriptions, accurate maps, and all the information necessary for enjoyable trips. You can order extra copies of this book and get information and prices for other Falcon guidebooks by writing Falcon, P.O. Box 1718, Helena, MT 59624 or calling toll free 1-800-582-2665. Also, please ask for a free copy of our current catalog. Visit our website at http://www.falconguide.com

©1998 by Falcon® Publishing Co., Inc., Helena, Montana.
A division of Landmark Guidebooks, Inc.

10 9 8 7 6 5 4 3 2 1

Falcon and FalconGuide are registered trademarks of Falcon Publishing Co., Inc.

Printed in Canada.

Cover photo by Chuck Haney.

Library of Congress Cataloging-in-Publication Data
    Peel, John
        Mountain Biking Durango / by John Peel
            p.   cm.
        Includes bibliographical references (p.).
        ISBN 1-56044-531-9 (pbk.)
        1. All terrain cycling—Colorado—Durango Region—Guidebooks.
    2. Durango Region (Colo.)—Guidebooks.   I. Title.
    GV1045.5.D87P44   1998
    917.88'29—dc21
97-50138
                                                                    CIP

CAUTION
        Outdoor recreational activities are by their very nature potentially hazardous. All participants in such activities must assume the responsibility for their own actions and safety. The information contained in this guidebook cannot replace sound judgment and good decision-making skills, which help reduce the risk exposure, nor does the scope of this book allow for disclosure of all the potential hazards and risks involved in such activities.
        Learn as much as possible about the outdoor recreational activities in which you participate, prepare for the unexpected, and be cautious. The reward will be a safer and more enjoyable experience.
♻ Text pages printed on recycled paper.

Contents

Acknowledgments v
USGS Topo Map Index vi
Map Legend viii
Durango City Map ix
Durango and West Map x
North of Durango Map xi
East of Durango Map xii
Foreword xiii
Preface xiv

Get Ready to CRANK!

The Durango Backcountry: What to Expect 2
Rules of the Trail 4
IMBA Rules of the Trail 5
How to Use this Guide 6
Rating the Rides 9
Aerobic Level Ratings 10
Elevation Graphs 12
Technical Difficulty Ratings 12
The Name Game 15
A Short Index of Rides 16

Around Durango

1   The Ridge 19
2   Chapman Hill Loop 22
3   Smelter Mountain 24
4   Log Chutes 27
5   Animas City Mountain 30

Colorado Trail near Durango

6   Dry Fork Loop 32
7   Colorado Trail–Hoffheins Connection 35
8   Colorado Trail from Sliderock Trail 39

La Plata Canyon

9   Kennebec Pass 42
10   Eagle Pass 46
11   The Notch 48

Mancos Area

12   Old Railroad Grade 51

13 Madden Peak 53
14 North Fork West Mancos Loop 55
15 Burnt Ridge Loop 61
16 Big West Mancos Loop 63
17 Chicken Creek 66

Hermosa Area

18 Hermosa Creek 70
19 Jones Creek to Mitchell Lakes 73
20 Elbert Creek to Jones Creek 76
21 Jones–Dutch–Hermosa Loop 79

Purgatory Area

22 Old Lime Creek Road 82
23 Harris Park Loop 85
24 Elbert Creek Loop 88
25 Cascade Loop 90
26 Cascade Divide to Relay Creek 94

Colorado Trail North

27 Molas to Coal Bank 98
28 Bolam Pass to Hotel Draw 102
29 Molas to Silverton 105

Silverton Area

30 Clear Lake 108
31 Placer to Picayne 111

Missionary Ridge

32 Haflin Creek 114
33 First Fork 118
34 Stevens Creek 121
35 Stevens to First Fork 123

East of Bayfield

36 Moonlick Park 126
37 Devil Mountain 130
38 Chris Mountain 132
39 Chris Mountain Big Loop 134

Appendix A: Other Durango-area Routes 137
Appendix B: Information Sources and Bike Shops 142
Glossary 144
About the Author 146

Acknowledgments

It started in the 1800s when early settlers built roads high into the San Juan Mountains, mainly searching for gold and silver. Thanks to these roads, and the roads and trails that followed in the next century, there are reams of good rides in the Durango area.

So here's a thanks to all those who built and maintained the trails on which we now ride our heavy-duty bikes, and a nod to those who continue to forge new trails and look after what we have.

A little closer to the heart, there were many who helped me see this project through. Foremost among them was Judy, who became my wife as I toiled on the book. She went on many of these rides with me, and if she ever thought she was a burden, I can assure her she was not.

Others helped me avoid long days alone on the trail, inspired me with ideas, and helped this mechanically challenged writer keep his bike in tune, sometimes in the middle of a ride.

Those include Rich Stewart, Mark Ritchey, Dean and Christina Howard, Shawna Off, Mike Skellion, John Glover, Bill Manning, and Susan Bagley, who waited in the car with a wound (which later took 11 stitches) while Judy and I completed a ride.

And thanks also go to my best man, Steve Chapman—hey, come out and do some of these fun rides with me sometime, huh?—his wife Carol, and my parents, who will get the first copy.

USGS
TOPO MAP INDEX

						Ophir
					Hermosa Peak	Engineer Mountain
			Wallace Ranch	Orphan Butte	Elk Creek	Electra Lake (550)
		Millwood	Rampart Hills	La Plata	Monument Hill	Hermosa / Hermosa
Cortez (160)	Mancos	Thompson Park	Hesperus	Durango West	Durango East / Durango
				Basin Mountain	Loma Linda (550)

TO FARMINGTON,
NEW MEXICO

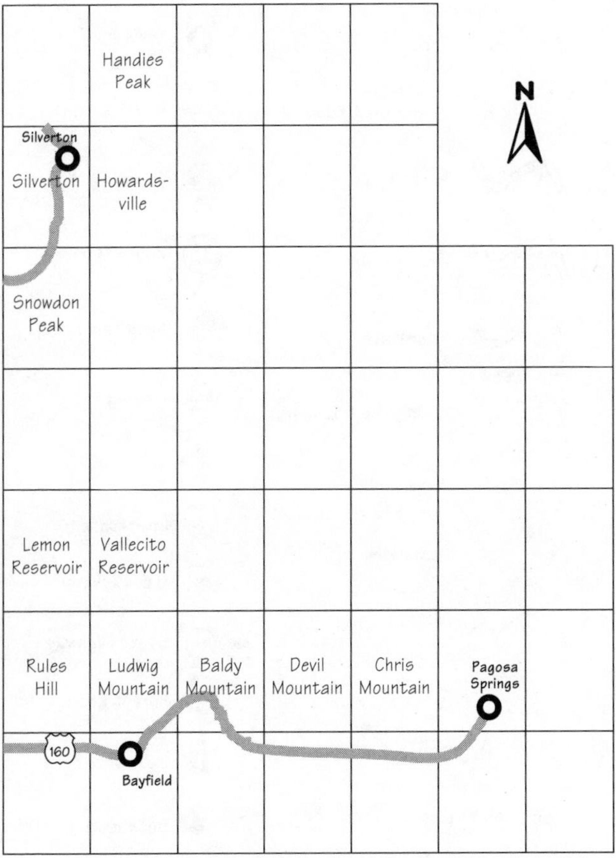

N
Handies Peak
Silverton
Silverton
Howardsville
Snowdon Peak
Lemon Reservoir
Vallecito Reservoir
Rules Hill
Ludwig Mountain
Baldy Mountain
Devil Mountain
Chris Mountain
Pagosa Springs
160
Bayfield

MAP LEGEND

 Trail

 Unimproved Road

 Paved Road

 Gravel Road

 Interstate

 Wilderness Boundary

 Waterway

 State Line

 Cliff

 Lake/Reservoir

 Slickrock

 Gate

 Picnic Area

 Restroom

 Town

 City

 Trailhead

 Route Marker

 Mountain Peak

 Parking

 Mile Marker

 Interstate

 U.S. Highway

 State Highway

 Forest Road

 Industrial Zone

 Building

Ruins

Camping

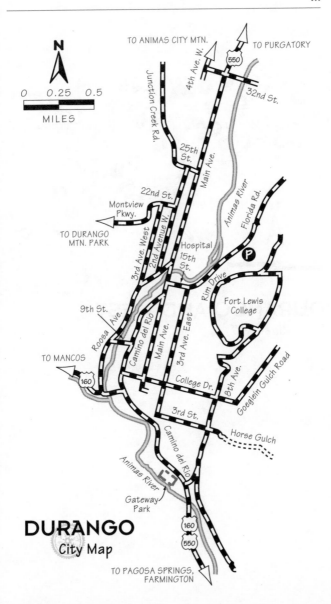

DURANGO
City Map

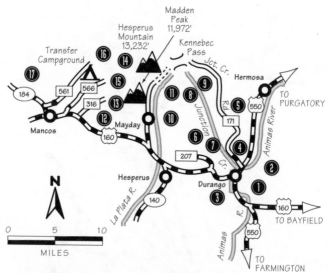

DURANGO AND WEST
Rides 1-17

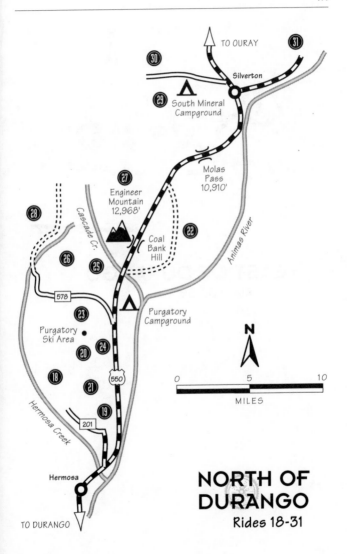

NORTH OF DURANGO

Rides 18-31

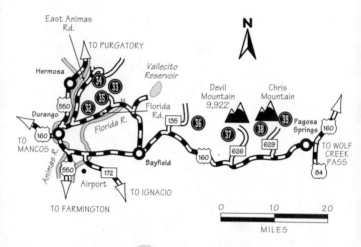

EAST OF DURANGO
Rides 32-39

Foreword

From high on rocky, mountainous trails down to the smooth rolling hills south of the border in New Mexico, Durango has it all in a beautiful setting of the San Juan Mountains.

Southwest Colorado is a playground I've enjoyed and explored for 16 years, and it seems there's always something new to try.

It's obviously an excellent training ground, and the wide variety of road and off-road rides, many at high altitude, have been a key to my success. By traveling just a little ways south of Durango, it's possible to ride almost year-around.

Whether you race or simply like to have fun, you should enjoy the rides in this book. Try the classics: the grunt up Animas City Mountain, The Ridge overlooking town, the high altitude of Kennebec Pass, or the smooth rolling hills of the Road Apple course in New Mexico. There's always something to challenge even the best rider.

Ned Overend,
1990 World Mountain Bike Champion
Six-time National Champion.

Preface

There's more to Durango than just one sport. People fly-fish in Durango. They kayak, they ski, they even play golf and tennis.

And there is a reason a slew of pro mountain bikers, and hundreds of amateur fat-tire enthusiasts, have chosen to make this area home.

Yes, there are many rides. A few are relatively easy, suitable for a beginner or sightseer. Many more are steep, rocky, long, and demanding. In general, the classic rides here are for those who enjoy being challenged, who like to sweat and grunt, who like to test the travel on their shock(s). Durango is a training ground for pros because the terrain keeps them sharp. It's also a training ground because even in winter there are places to ride—maybe not in Colorado and maybe not off-road. But more on that later.

Beyond the terrain, there is the challenge of procuring oxygen, which lowlanders often find difficult. Locals enjoy watching first-time area riders, who assume they're ready for the Durango experience, bonk early and often. Some survive, though humbled.

OK, it's not really that difficult. Just don't take your first ride with Ned Overend or John Tomac. Go easy. Go at your own pace. Don't ride what looks like sure death. Get off and walk. Don't try to keep up with the natives on the downhills. They know the trails, and some of them do this for a living.

Enjoy!

John Peel,
Durango

Get Ready to CRANK!

Welcome to *Mountain Biking Durango*. Here are 39 rides for the beginner and top expert. Already psyched out by Durango's reputed gonzo mentality? Relax. Don't worry that you don't have front and rear suspension, ceramic rims, or clipless pedals. If you're not a racer, that's fine. Many of us don't race. We still enjoy the sport, perhaps even more.

The rides are described in plain language, with accurate distances and ratings for physical and technical difficulty. Each entry offers a wealth of detailed information that's easy to read and use, from an armchair or on the trail.

Our aim here is three-fold: to help you choose a ride that's appropriate for your fitness and skill level; to make it easy to find the trailhead; and to help you complete the ride safely, without getting lost. Take care of these basics and fun is bound to break loose.

The Durango Backcountry: What to Expect

The rides in this book cover a wide variety of terrain. But most of the rides are mountainous and that means two things: they are steep and rough, and weather can be unpredictable—at times severe.

Mountain terrain requires preparedness. Get in good shape before you attempt any of these rides, and know your limits. Keep your bike running smoothly with frequent cleaning and maintenance. Make sure everything's tight. Check out that strange clicking sound before you go on that all-day, 30-mile backcountry ride.

Always carry at least one water bottle (and don't forget to fill it). A snack, such as fruit or a sports energy bar, will help provide a lift during a long ride. Dress for the weather and pack a wind- and water-proof jacket whenever there's any doubt. Clouds and rain come out of nowhere in the mountains. It can get cold really fast. Don't forget sunglasses, sunscreen, lip balm, and insect repellent, as needed.

For tools, have at minimum a spare tube, patch kit, and pump. You can rely on a companion for a pump, but it's much better to carry your own. Carry a small kit including screwdriver, chain tool, and appropriate allen wrenches. Keep in mind that different bikes need different tools.

Do you value your head? Wear a helmet. Cycling gloves are another essential piece of safety equipment—saving hands from cuts and bruises from falls and encroaching branches and rocks. They also improve your grip and comfort on the handlebars. Eyewear seems essential to me; UV rays are strong at high altitudes, and sunglasses can protect your eyes from branches, twigs, and even rocks.

This book is designed to be easily carried along in a jersey pocket or fanny pack, and the maps and ride descriptions will help anyone unfamiliar with the trails. For a more detailed picture of the terrain, scan a U.S. Geological Survey topographic map beforehand (although ride routes are not always shown). The correct maps are listed in the at-a-glance information for each ride. A compass and bike computer help greatly in following the ride descriptions.

Durango area **weather** is unstable. It snows in May and June, but it can be sunny and dry in January. In midsummer, trails around town can be extremely hot. So bring lots of water and a jacket—preferably waterproof. If you are driving to a trailhead, play it safe and take a variety of clothes in the car to match the variable weather you may encounter.

At any time of year rain or snow can turn trails to purée for days afterward. Please stay off wet, muddy trails. The risk of soil damage and erosion is simply too great. Another "hazard" that can't be avoided is cow pies. Close your lips tightly in sections where they abound in fresh piles, and try not to get any on your hands. You don't want any bovine microbes (such as *Giardia lamblia*) going from hand to mouth.

Good off-road riding in the Durango vicinity is available from at least April through November, sometimes sooner and sometimes later. But the good, long, high-altitude rides must be done from mid-June through September. Some trails, particularly at higher elevations, have even shorter seasons running from late July through August. (Big-game hunting season runs from mid-October through mid-November. Check locally and wear orange if you ride at this time. Archery and muzzleloading seasons begin in August, but these seasons are generally much safer.)

Which trails can be ridden at what time of year varies widely. In some years, snow in the high country falls as rain in town. Hermosa Creek, a highlight ride, should be open by June, but inquire locally. High water levels can make it dangerous. Rides that go above 10,000 feet, such as the Molas Pass to

Silverton route, may not be totally rideable until mid-July. In town, The Ridge can be ridden all year sometimes, although there are shady sections with ice to be wary of.

In winter, it's easier to pick up a new sport than try to battle conditions. Cross-country skiing is available in town in decent snow years, and downhill area skiing is half an hour away. If this is starting to sound like a chamber of commerce ad, then bag the ski area and hit the backcountry. (Inquire about the avalanche danger, of course.)

Rules of the Trail

I must admit that when I'm a hiker, mountain bikers bug me. I want to relax and enjoy the scenery, not worry about some machine running me over. I cringe when seeing off-road riders take the right-of-way away, not bothering to yield when they should.

So please treat hikers and horseback riders with respect. The rule—yeah, I know, we all love to be anarchists—is to yield to both. Do so. Even if you are *training* for a race, you're not *in* a race. You can take five or fifteen or even thirty seconds to get out of the way. With horses, try to get below them; if you're above them, they may think you are a predator and you are going to pounce on them.

Most mountain bikers are conscientious and are trying to do the right thing. Most of us don't need rules. But we do need knowledge. What exactly *is* the right thing to do?

Here are some guidelines, reprinted by permission from the International Mountain Bicycling Association (IMBA).

IMBA Rules of the Trail

Thousands of miles of dirt trails have been closed to mountain bicyclists. The irresponsible riding habits of a few riders have been a factor. Do your part to maintain trail access by observing the following rules of the trail, formulated by the International Mountain Bicycling Association (IMBA). IMBA's mission is to promote environmentally sound and socially responsible mountain biking.

1. Ride on open trails only. Respect trail and road closures (ask if not sure), avoid possible trespass on private land, obtain permits and authorization as may be required. Federal and state wilderness areas are closed to cycling. The way you ride will influence trail management decisions and policies.

2. Leave no trace. Be sensitive to the dirt beneath you. Even on open (legal) trails, you should not ride under conditions where you will leave evidence of your passing, such as on certain soils after a rain. Recognize different types of soil and trail construction; practice low-impact cycling. This also means staying on existing trails and not creating any new ones. Be sure to pack out at least as much as you pack in.

3. Control your bicycle! Inattention for even a second can cause problems. Obey all bicycle speed regulations and recommendations.

4. Always yield trail. Make known your approach well in advance. A friendly greeting (or bell) is considerate and works well; don't startle others. Show your respect when passing by slowing to a walking pace or even stopping. Anticipate other trail users around corners or in blind spots.

5. Never spook animals. All animals are startled by an unannounced approach, a sudden movement, or a loud noise. This can be dangerous for you, others, and the animals. Give animals extra room and time to adjust to you. When passing horses use special care and follow directions from the horseback riders (ask if uncertain). Running cattle and disturbing wildlife is a serious offense. Leave gates as you found them, or as marked.

6. Plan ahead. Know your equipment, your ability, and the area in which you are riding—and prepare accordingly. Be self-sufficient at all times, keep your equipment in good repair, and carry necessary supplies for changes in weather or other conditions. A well-executed trip is a satisfaction to you and not a burden or offense to others. Always wear a helmet. For more information: Jim Hasenauer, Director of Education, International Mountain Bicycling Association, IMBAJim@aol.com

How to Use this Guide

Mountain Biking Durango describes 39 mountain bike rides in their entirety. A handful of other local routes, including some of the best rides right around town, are mentioned briefly in Appendix A.

Twenty-six of the featured rides are loops, beginning and ending at the same point but coming and going on different trails. Loops are by far the most popular type of ride, and that thought was in mind when this book was written. Portions of some rides follow gravel and even paved roads, and a handful of rides never touch a trail.

Be forewarned, however: the difficulty of a loop ride may change dramatically depending on which direction you ride around the loop. If you are unfamiliar with the rides in this book, try them first as described here. The directions follow the path of least resistance (which does not necessarily mean "easy"). After you've been over the terrain, you can determine whether a given loop would be fun—or even feasible—in the reverse direction.

Each ride description in this book follows the same format:

Number and Name of the Ride: Rides are cross-referenced by number throughout this book. In many cases, parts of rides or entire routes can be linked to other rides for longer trips or variations on a standard route. These opportunities are noted, followed by "see Ride(s) #."

For the names of rides I relied on official names of trails, roads, and natural features as shown on national forest and U.S. Geological Survey maps. In some cases deference was given to long-term local custom, as in "The Ridge," which is unlabeled on some maps.

Location: The general whereabouts of the ride; distance and direction from Durango.

Distance: The length of the ride in miles, given as a loop, one way, or round trip.

Time: An estimate of how long it takes to complete the ride, for example, 1 to 2 hours. *The time listed is the actual riding time and* *does not include rest stops.* Strong, skilled riders may be able to do a given ride in less than the estimated time, while other riders may take considerably longer. Also bear in mind that severe weather, changes in trail conditions, or mechanical problems may prolong a ride.

Tread: The type of road or trail: paved road, gravel road, dirt road, four-wheel-drive road, doubletrack, ATV-width singletrack, and singletrack.

Aerobic level: The level of physical effort required to complete the ride: easy, moderate, or strenuous. (See the explanation of the rating systems on page 10).

Technical difficulty: The level of bike handling skills needed to complete the ride upright and in one piece. Technical difficulty is rated on a scale from 1 to 5, with 1 being the easiest and 5 the hardest (see the explanation of the rating systems on page 12).

Hazards: A list of dangers that may be encountered on a ride, including traffic, weather, trail obstacles and conditions, risky stream crossings, difficult route-finding, and other perils. Remember: conditions may change at any time. Be alert for storms, new fences, downfall, missing trail signs, and mechanical failure. Fatigue, heat, cold, and/or dehydration may impair judgment.

Highlights: Special features or qualities that make a ride worth doing (as if we needed an excuse!): fun singletrack, long downhills, and more, including scenery, which could be included in every ride highlight.

Land status: A list of managing agencies or land owners. Most of the rides in this book are on the San Juan National Forest. But some rides also cross portions of private, state, or municipal lands. Always leave gates as you found them. And respect the land, regardless of who owns it. Please obey all no trespassing signs and obtain permission before crossing private property. See Appendix B for a list of local addresses for land-managing agencies.

Maps: A list of available maps. The San Juan National Forest visitors' map (scaled at 1:126,720) affords a good overview of travel routes in the region. USGS topographic maps (scaled 1:24,000) in the 7.5-minute quad series provide a close-up look at terrain. Many routes are not shown on official maps.

Access: How to find the trailhead or the start of the ride. A number of rides can be pedaled right from town; for others it's best to drive to the trailhead.

The ride: A mile-by-mile list of key points—landmarks, notable climbs and descents, stream crossings, obstacles, hazards, major turns and junctions—along the ride. All distances were measured to the tenth of a mile with a cyclo-computer (a bike-mounted odometer). Terrain, riding technique, and tire pressure can affect odometer readings, so treat all mileages as estimates. I found on steep trails that going up measured longer than coming down—and it seemed like it too.

Finally, one last reminder that the real world is changing all the time. The information presented here is as accurate and up-to-date as possible, but there are no guarantees out in the mountains. You alone are responsible for your safety and for the choices you make on the trail.

If you do find an error or omission in this book, or a new and noteworthy change in the field, I'd like to hear from you. Please write to John Peel, c/o Falcon Publishing, P.O. Box 1718, Helena, MT 59624, or send e-mail to: falcon@desktop.org.

Rating the Rides

Rating a ride is tricky, because everyone's scale is different. And a ride is more difficult when done faster, and more dangerous when technical sections are ridden instead of walked.

One of the first lessons learned by most mountain bikers is to not trust their friends' accounts of how easy or difficult a given ride may be.

"It's not bad," they say, "just a few rollers." But that may mean several 500-foot climbs along a highly technical ridge. (I learned that on Ride 28.)

So how do you know what you're getting into, before it's too late?

Don't always listen to your friends. But do read this book. There is enough information in here for you to make a good assessment of your ability and each ride's difficulty.

Falcon mountain biking guides rate each ride for two types of difficulty: the *physical effort* required to pedal the distance, and the level of *bike-handling skills* needed to stay upright and make it home in one piece. We call these **Aerobic level** and **Technical difficulty.**

The following sections explain what the various ratings mean in plain, specific language. An elevation profile accompanies each ride description to help you determine how easy or hard the ride is. Also weigh other factors such as elevation above sea level, total trip distance, weather and wind, and current trail conditions. And, of course, who you're riding with.

Aerobic Level Ratings

Bicycling is often touted as a relaxing, low-impact, relatively easy way to burn excess calories and maintain a healthy heart and lungs. Mountain biking, however, tends to pack a little more work (and excitement) into the routine.

Fat tires and soft or rough trails increase the rolling resistance, so it takes more effort to push those wheels around. And unpaved or off-road hills tend to be steeper than grades measured and tarred by the highway department. When we use the word *steep*, we mean a sweat-inducing, oxygen-sucking, lactose-building climb. If it's followed by an exclamation point—steep (!)—expect some honest pain on the way up (and maybe for days afterward).

So expect to breathe hard and sweat some, probably a lot. Pedaling the paved roads around town is a good start, but it won't fully prepare you for the workout offered by most of the rides in this book. If you're unsure of your fitness level, see a doctor for a physical exam. And if you're riding to get back in shape or just for the fun of it, take it easy. Walk or rest if need be. Start with short rides and add on miles gradually.

Here's how we rate the exertion level for terrain covered in this book:

Easy: Flat or gently rolling terrain. No steeps or prolonged climbs.

Moderate: Some hills. Climbs may be short and fairly steep or long and gradual.

Strenuous: Frequent or prolonged climbs steep enough to require riding in the lowest gear; requires a high level of aerobic fitness, power, and endurance (typically acquired through many hours of riding and proper training). Less fit riders may need to walk.

Many rides are mostly easy and moderate but may have short strenuous sections. Other rides are mostly strenuous and should be attempted only after a complete medical checkup and implant of a second heart, preferably a *big* one. One mile on a rough trail with downed timber can wear you out much quicker than 10 miles on a smooth trail. Good riding skills and a relaxed stance on the bike save energy.

Finally, any ride can be strenuous if you ride it hard and fast. Conversely, the pain of a lung-burning climb grows easier to tolerate as your fitness level improves. Learn to pace yourself.

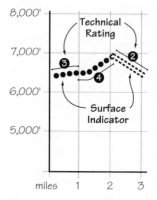

Elevation Graphs

An elevation profile accompanies each ride description. Here the ups and downs of the route are graphed on a grid of elevation (in feet above sea level) on the left and miles pedaled across the bottom. Route surface conditions (see map legend), and technical levels are shown as well.

Note that these graphs are compressed to fit on the page. The actual slopes are not as steep as the lines drawn on the graphs, even though it may feel that way. Also, some short dips and climbs are too small to show up on the graphs. Any major grade change, however, will be mentioned in the ride description.

Technical Difficulty Ratings

Some trails, especially near town, are "dialed in." They're ridden constantly, and stray rocks have long since been pushed out of the way by a speeding tire. The tread is smooth and predictable. Enjoy these trails.

One day I set out to explore a trail I found on the San Juan National Forest map north of Mancos. The trail got rougher and rougher, with barely rideable rocky sections, places where the bike had to be pushed, and then places where the bike had to be carried because the trail was too narrow to push it. After about 10 miles of this, I was exhausted and nearly in tears. Finally, to my great relief, I came to a familiar road I knew would complete the loop.

So, what does this have to do with technical ratings? It's common sense that the technical difficulty of a trail adds to its relative "length." Furthermore, a difficult trail can make an advanced rider feel like a beginner and a beginner feel like he or she should be playing badminton.

Of all the information in this book, the technical rating is probably the most important. There is always a danger in mountain biking, but that danger can be minimized by riding trails that suit your ability. If you hesitate before a technical section, say a steep drop with loose boulders, you probably shouldn't be riding it.

The technical difficulty ratings help take the worst surprises out of backcountry rides. In the privacy of your own home you can make an honest appraisal of your bike-handling skills and then find rides in these pages within your ability.

We rate technical difficulty on a scale from 1 to 5, from easiest to most difficult. We tried to make the ratings as objective as possible by considering the type of obstacles and their frequency of occurrence. The same standards were applied consistently through all the rides in this book.

We've also added plus (+) and minus (-) symbols to cover gray areas between given levels of difficulty: a 4+ obstacle is harder than a 4, but easier than a 5-. A stretch of trail rated as 5+ would be unrideable by all but the most skilled (or luckiest) riders.

Here are the five levels defined:

Level 1: Smooth tread; road or doubletrack; no obstacles, ruts, or steeps. Requires basic bike-riding skills.

Level 2: Mostly smooth tread; wide, well-groomed singletrack or road/doubletrack with minor ruts or loose gravel or sand.

Level 3: Irregular tread with some rough sections; single or doubletrack with obvious route choices; some steep sections; occasional obstacles may include small rocks, roots, water bars, ruts, loose gravel or sand, and sharp turns or broad, open switchbacks.

Level 4: Rough tread with few smooth places; singletrack or rough doubletrack with limited route choices; steep sections, some with obstacles; obstacles are numerous and varied, including rocks, roots, branches, ruts, sidehills, narrow tread, loose gravel or sand, and switchbacks.

Level 5: Continuously broken, rocky, root-infested, or trenched tread; singletrack or extremely rough doubletrack with few route choices; frequent, sudden, and severe changes in gradient; some slopes so steep that wheels lift off ground; obstacles are nearly continuous and may include boulders, logs, water, large holes, deep ruts, ledges, piles of loose gravel, steep sidehills, encroaching trees, and tight switchbacks.

Again, most of the rides in this book cover varied terrain, with an ever-changing degree of technical difficulty. Some trails run smooth with only occasional obstacles, and other trails are seemingly all obstacle. The path of least resistance, or *line*, is where you find it. In general, most obstacles are more challenging if you encounter them while climbing than while descending. On the other hand, in heavy surf (e.g., boulder fields, tangles of downfall, cliffs), fear plays a larger role when facing downhill.

Realize, too, that different riders have different strengths and weaknesses. Some folks can scramble over logs and boulders without a grunt, but they crash head over heels on every switchback turn. Some fly off the steepest drops and others freeze. Some riders climb like the wind and others just blow . . . and walk.

The key to overcoming "technical difficulties" is practice: keep trying. Follow a rider who makes it look easy, and don't hesitate to ask for constructive criticism. Try shifting your weight (good riders move a lot, front to back, side to side, and up and down) and experimenting with balance and momentum. Practice balancing at a standstill in a "track stand" (described in the Glossary). This will give you more confidence—and more time to recover or bail out—the next time the trail rears up and bites.

The Name Game

If you spend a lot of time in Durango, you may hear of trails named "Stonehenge," "Suicide," and "Star Wars."

These nicknames may help to distinguish or describe certain parts of the overall ride—but only for the group of people that knows the nickname.

For the sake of clarity, I stuck to the official (or at least most widely accepted) names for the trails and roads described in this book. Where a route is commonly known by more than one name, the other names are mentioned. If you know the local routes by some other name, or if you come up with nicknames that peg the personalities of these rides, then by all means share them with your riding buddies.

A Short Index of Rides

Marginally Mellow—Easier Rides
3. Smelter Mountain
12. Old Railroad Grade
15. Burnt Ridge Loop
17. Chicken Creek
22. Old Lime Creek Road
23. Harris Park Loop

Sweet Singletrack—Rides with a High Percentage of Singletrack
6. Dry Fork Loop
8. CT from Sliderock Trail
18. Hermosa Creek
20. Elbert Creek to Jones Creek
21. Jones/Dutch/Hermosa Loop
27. Molas to Coal Bank
28. Bolam to Hotel Draw
29. Molas to Silverton
33. First Fork
35. Stevens to First Fork

Endless Climbs (Or, Where's the Top?)
5. Animas City Mountain
9. Kennebec Pass
10. Eagle Pass
11. The Notch
13. Madden Peak
19. Jones Creek to Mitchell Lakes
28. Bolam to Hotel Draw
30. Clear Lake
31. Placer to Picayne Loop
32. Haflin Creek

33. First Fork
35. Stevens to First Fork

Mountain Madness—Trails to a Summit
3. Smelter Mountain
5. Animas City Mountain
13. Madden Peak
37. Devil Mountain
38. Chris Mountain Loop

In the Clouds—Rides Above Timberline
9. Kennebec Pass
10. Eagle Pass
11. The Notch
13. Madden Peak
26. Cascade Divide to Relay Creek Loop
27. Molas to Coal Bank
28. Bolam to Hotel Draw
29. Molas to Silverton
30. Clear Lake
31. Placer to Picayne Loop

Fast and Fun—Downhills That Make You Smile
4. Log Chutes
5. Animas City Mountain
6. Dry Fork Loop
7. CT/Hoffheins Connection
18. Hermosa Creek
20. Elbert Creek to Jones Creek
28. Bolam to Hotel Draw
31. Placer to Picayne Loop
35. Stevens to First Fork
39. Chris Mountain Big Loop

Too Technical?—Rough and Rocky Routes

5. Animas City Mountain
21. Jones/Dutch/Hermosa Loop
27. Molas to Coal Bank
28. Bolam to Hotel Draw
29. Molas to Silverton
32. Haflin Creek
33. First Fork
35. Stevens to First Fork

The Ridge

Location: From town, east along Horse Gulch Road and up to The Ridge overlooking Fort Lewis College.

Distance: 5.2-mile loop.

Time: 30 minutes to 1 hour.

Tread: 1.7 miles on rough dirt road; 1.9 miles on technical four-wheel-drive road; 1.6 miles on rocky singletrack.

Aerobic level: Strenuous, with steep climbs.

Technical difficulty: A lot of 4, some 5.

Hazards: The Ridge section has several short steep drops and rocky technical sections. Make sure quick-release pedals are working. (Mine weren't one day, and I have the scars to prove it.) Those with full suspension will enjoy this ride. Most of the way the main path is fairly obvious thanks to the tracks of local riders.

Highlights: Easy access, good workout, nice views of town.

Land status: County road, Fort Lewis College Foundation.

Map: USGS Durango East.

Access: From downtown Durango go to the southeast edge of town to the intersection of 8th Avenue and 3rd Street. Go east on 3rd Street, which turns into Horse Gulch Road in one block. Parking is limited; visitors with cars may want to park elsewhere in town.

1. THE RIDGE
2. CHAPMAN HILL
LOOP

The ride:

0.0 Head east up Horse Gulch Road, climbing fairly steeply. Pass a couple of spur roads on the left.

0.7 Pass a dirt road on the right that leads to the Telegraph Trail (see Appendix A).

1.0 Make a 120-degree turn left onto a four-wheel-drive road, momentarily heading west. The really steep climb begins.

1.1   Veer right at a Y junction, heading north and uphill.

1.5   Pooped out? Take a left and go up the black dirt to the top of The Ridge. Skip to mile 3.4 below. For those doing the full ride, veer right on the four-wheel-drive road, which doesn't get any less rocky. Soon begin a rocky uphill to the top of The Ridge.

2.4   Crest the top of The Ridge. Enjoy views of Hillcrest Golf Club, the city, and the La Plata Mountains to the west. From here, find the trail going west and uphill on The Ridge. (Don't take the trail heading east.) A steep, sometimes rideable rocky section leads to a fairly flat, rocky section. Eventually the trail goes slightly down-hill; watch for tricky dropoffs.

3.4   Note the black dirt on the left and the road you came up on. Meet riding companions who pooped out here.

4.0   The trail spills out onto another four-wheel-drive road. Go left (east). Bike tracks should make it obvious where to go. The road goes downhill east, and in 0.2 mile swings back around to the west.

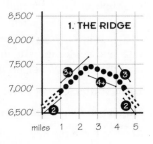

4.5   After a short, steep drop, you'll be a few yards from Horse Gulch Road. Turn left and return to Horse Gulch. Then go right and downhill (west).

5.2   Welcome back to the starting point.

Chapman Hill Loop

[See map on page 20]

Location: Durango city limits, at Chapman Hill Ski Area.

Distance: 2.2-mile loop.

Time: 15 to 25 minutes.

Tread: 1.6 miles on doubletrack; 0.6 mile on wide singletrack.

Aerobic level: Strenuous, because of the Chapman Hill climb.

Technical difficulty: 3.

Hazards: Stray golf balls, possible two-way traffic.

Highlights: A fun downhill with switchbacks. This ride, combined with Horse Gulch, makes up the Iron Horse Bicycle Classic race course. Because some of the Iron Horse course is on private land it was not written up in this guide. Consult a local bike shop for current land status of the race course.

Land status: City of Durango and Fort Lewis College.

Maps: San Juan National Forest; USGS Durango East.

Access: From the intersection of 15th Street and East 3rd Avenue, take Florida Road northeast 0.5 mile to the Chapman Hill Ski Area parking lot.

The ride:

0.0   Look up the ski hill to the green shack on top, with a couple of road cuts leading up to it from the left. That's our destination. Are you sure you want to work this hard? The best way to start is to follow a zig-zag course up, starting out on the right and slowly veering left (east) in the first 0.1 mile, ending up on a very short singletrack section that leads to an old road.

0.2   If you're on target, you should be turning right at about this point on an old road, beginning the final, long climb to the top. It's a challenge, but you can ride it!

0.4   Reach the top, rejoice, and turn left (east) onto singletrack just below paved Rim Drive, which circles campus. The trail is a wide track that stays just below Rim Drive.

0.8   A short uphill rises to the level of Rim Drive. Follow the singletrack on the left side of the road next to Hillcrest Golf Course.

1.0   Just past the golf course clubhouse, take a left (north) uphill off the road, again on doubletrack.

1.1   Pass close to the Lion's Den, a small pavilion, and start downhill. Begin a series of hairpin turns on this fun descent.

2.1   With the skating rink in sight, veer left up a short hill. In 40 yards, go down through a fun set of "S"-turns. Go left around the rink.

2.2   Return to the parking lot. Another lap?

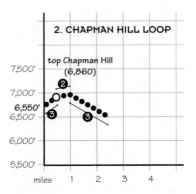

Smelter Mountain

Location: South of town on Smelter Mountain, a resting place for TV towers and radio antennae above Durango.

Distance: 8.2 miles out-and-back.

Time: 45 minutes to 2 hours.

Tread: 4.6 miles on gravel road; 3.6 miles on dirt road.

Aerobic level: Moderate, with some short strenuous sections.

Technical difficulty: 1 and 2.

Hazards: Watch for traffic, especially on County Road 211. If the hotly debated Animas–La Plata dam is built, the traffic will increase greatly. During the summer it's very hot with little shade.

Highlights: A good early season ride—close to town, a good workout, and nice views.

Land status: County roads surrounded by Colorado Division of Wildlife land.

Maps: USGS Durango West, Basin Mountain.

Access: From the intersection of Camino del Rio and U.S. Highway 160 in Durango, go 1.2 miles south on Camino del Rio (U.S. Highway 550/160). Turn right at the first traffic light after crossing the Animas River (which is past Gateway Park and well before the Durango Mall). In 50 yards take another right onto CR 211 and park along the shoulder of the road.

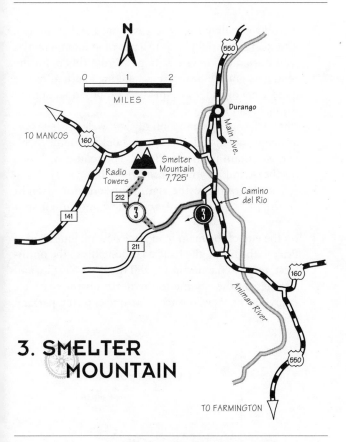

3. SMELTER
MOUNTAIN

The ride:

0.0   Head west uphill on gravel CR 211.

1.6   Pass a power station on the north side of road.

1.8   Reach a junction, which is also a topping-out point on
      CR 211. Take a right on CR 212 and continue up a
      slight grade. (CR 211 continues down into Ridges Ba-
      sin.)

2.3   A road veers off to the right (east), but stay left (north). The road to the right leads to a pile of uranium tailings, well-buried by crews (we hope). From this point the road gets granny-gear steep. Looking south affords a good view of Ridges Basin—the proposed site of the Animas–La Plata dam.

3.0   The road tops out momentarily and welcome shade is available under a tall ponderosa. Look north to see Silver Mountain in the La Platas. The road now heads northeast and TV towers soon come into view.

3.8   A road takes off to the right, but continue straight (north) to road's end. A good view and lunch spot awaits.

4.1   It's the end of the main road. The view includes Perins Peak to the north, the La Plata Mountains to the northwest, town to the northeast, and the West Needles and Needles on the skyline to the north-northeast. After enjoying the view, retrace your tracks to the parking spot.

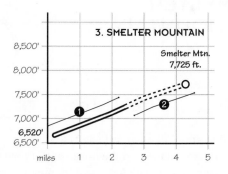

Log Chutes
[See map on page 29]

Location: Northwest of Durango above Junction Creek.

Distance: 6.4-mile loop (4.8 miles for a shorter variation).

Time: 1 to 1.5 hours.

Tread: 1.2 miles on four-wheel-drive road; 5.2 miles on abandoned logging roads and chutes that basically qualify as singletrack.

Aerobic level: Moderate.

Technical difficulty: Ranges from 2 to 4+.

Hazards: The downhill section is steep and can have treacherous ruts and jumps.

Highlights: A nice ride close to town and with a good uphill workout and a downhill that generates smiles.

Land status: San Juan National Forest.

Maps: San Juan National Forest; USGS Durango West.

Access: From Main Avenue in Durango go west on 25th Street, which becomes Junction Creek Road (County Road 204). In 3.5 miles the road crosses a cattle guard and becomes gravel. From there it is 2.2 miles to the Log Chutes trail parking lot on the east (right) side of road.

The ride:

0.0 Pedal east on a four-wheel-drive road. It rollercoasters for a while, but overall goes uphill.

1.2 Turn left off the road and go around a gate onto an abandoned road. Go north and uphill.

1.8 The turnoff for a shorter loop goes west on singletrack. For the long loop continue north another 50 yards and veer left (northwest) onto singletrack. (To follow the short loop, go 2.2 miles on a rocky trail with short climbs, not as well maintained as the long loop. Cross Junction Creek Road and continue on the trail. In another 0.1 mile join the long loop coming from the right at an old corral—at mile 5.7 below.)

2.1 The top of the climb. For the next 1.6 miles the trail goes up and down through a ponderosa/scrub oak forest.

3.0 Pass a swamp on the right (north).

3.7 Veer right (north) off the abandoned four-wheel-drive road you've been on and head uphill on nice singletrack. In the fall, this section has colorful aspen.

4.1 Cross Junction Creek Road and find the trail on the west side heading briefly north. Go 50 yards until the

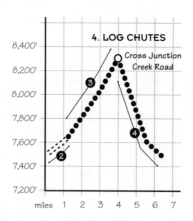

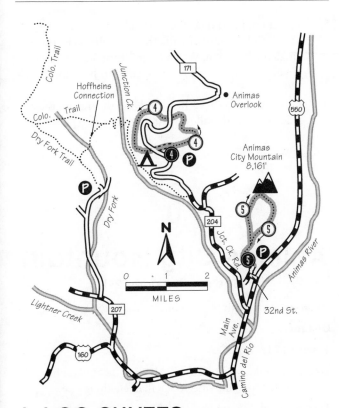

4. LOG CHUTES
5. ANIMAS CITY MOUNTAIN

trail meets a road coming from above. Head south on the road, going steeply downhill and giving the brakes a severe test.

4.8   The trail momentarily flattens out, giving your braking fingers a rest and offering a nice view west of Lewis Mountain in the La Platas.

5.7 Pass an old corral on the west side of the trail.

5.8 Turn right (south) off the doubletrack onto a singletrack section. Watch for this turn; it's easy to miss. If you do miss it you're dumped onto Junction Creek Road.

6.4 Cross Junction Creek Road and find the trail on the east side of the road. Follow it 100 yards back to parking lot.

Animas City Mountain
[See map on page 29]

Location: Just north of town on Animas City Mountain.

Distance: 5.9-mile loop.

Time: 1 to 1.5 hours.

Tread: 5.9 miles on singletrack. Much of the trail is on an old road, but it's more like singletrack than anything else.

Aerobic level: Strenuous.

Technical difficulty: Mostly 3+ and 4.

Hazards: The downhill section is very rocky and steep. In midsummer this ride can be hot. This trail gets lots of traffic; watch for hikers, dogs, and other bikers and yield the right of way.

Highlights: Views of town and surrounding area. This ride offers a great workout and good downhill test. If you feel good after this ride, you're in great shape.

Land status: Bureau of Land Management. (This trail is closed when big game are present between December 1 and April 15.)

Maps: San Juan National Forest; USGS Durango East.

Access: From Main Avenue in Durango, go west and uphill on 32nd Street, and take a right on West 4th Avenue. Continue to the dead end and a small parking lot.

The ride:

0.0   Trails are marked blue for mountain bikes and white for hikers. For the first section, ignore this and follow the white arrows going uphill, climbing through several steep switchbacks.

0.3   Go left (west) at a trail junction, now following blue arrows.

0.4   Reach an old road and go right (north) and uphill. From here the climb is steep for the next 2.2 miles.

0.7   Enjoy a view of the La Platas, with Silver Mountain the obvious peak. A hiking trail goes right (east) here, but continue the grunt straight (north) and uphill. In another 40 yards come to a junction and continue on the main trail veering left. The right-hand fork is the one on which you'll return.

2.0   Come to a short, flat section through a clearing. Ahh!!

2.6   Your reward: the north end of the mesa on Animas City Mountain,

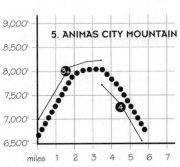

with excellent views all around. When you catch your breath, continue east on the trail, which has one more immediate steep section in store.

3.2   Roll onto the east end of the mesa. From here it's all downhill. The trail heads southeast on a rocky descent.

3.4   Veer right at the "Y" junction, following the blue arrow. Cross the hiking trail at miles 3.8 and 4.2.

5.2   The trail dumps out onto the one you came up on (at 0.7 mile). Retrace your tracks to the parking lot.

5.9   The trailhead, with the parking lot 50 yards beyond.

Dry Fork Loop

Location: A short distance west of Durango in the San Juan National Forest.

Distance: 9.2-mile loop.

Time: 1 to 1.5 hours.

Tread: 8.3 miles on singletrack; 0.9 mile on abandoned road.

Aerobic level: Moderate, with a long but not too difficult climb.

Technical difficulty: Mostly 3, some 4.

Hazards: The track can be rough if cattle have been grazing.

Highlights: Basically all singletrack! Fun downhill section.

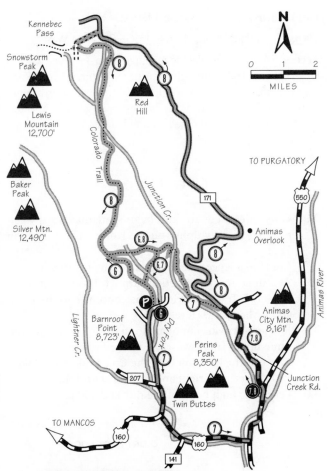

6. DRY FORK LOOP
7. COLORADO TRAIL—HOFFHEINS
CONNNECTION
8. COLORADO TRAIL FROM
SLIDEROCK TRAIL

Land status: San Juan National Forest.

Maps: San Juan National Forest; USGS Durango West.

Access: From Camino del Rio in Durango go 3.4 miles west on U.S. Highway 160. Turn right (north) on Lightner Creek Road (County Road 207). Go 1.1 miles and turn right (north) onto a dirt road (Dry Fork Road). In 2 miles veer right at a "Y" intersection. Go another 0.9 mile and pull left into a small parking area at the trailhead.

The ride:

0.0   Cross a cattleguard and begin pedaling northwest, heading slightly uphill on the Hoffheins Connection Trail.

0.7   Come to a fence; use the handy stairs to cross it.

0.9   At a three-way intersection turn left (northwest) onto Dry Fork Trail. The Hoffheins continues to the right, and is the way we'll return.

3.4   Join an old road coming up from the left (south). Continue uphill (northwest) on marked track.

4.3   Come to the junction with the Colorado Trail. Make a 120-degree turn right and climb a short hill.

4.6   Reach the high point of the ride at 8,650 feet.

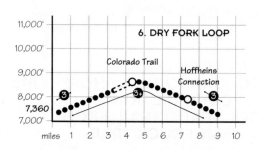

7.0   Take a right (south) off the Colorado Trail onto the Hoffheins Connection Trail. (Or, for a great view, ride 0.2 mile farther down the Colorado Trail to Gudy's Rest, then return to this junction with the Hoffheins Trail.)

8.3   Hit the three-way intersection (at 0.9 mile above). Veer left, continuing downhill on the Hoffheins Trail.

9.2   Return to the parking area.

Colorado Trail–Hoffheins Connection

[See map on page 33]

Location: North and west of Durango in the San Juan National Forest.

Distance: 17.6-mile loop. (22.6-mile loop with Dry Fork option.)

Time: 1.5 to 3 hours. (2 to 3.5 hours with Dry Fork option.)

Tread: 8 miles on paved road; 2.9 miles on dirt road; 6.7 miles on singletrack. (The Dry Fork option adds 4.1 miles on singletrack and 0.9 mile on an abandoned road.)

Aerobic level: Strenuous, with a 1.6-mile granny-gear climb.

Technical difficulty: Mostly 3, some 4.

Hazards: The trail can be busy, especially on weekends. Watch for horses and hikers, especially on blind corners. Also, County

Road 204 (Junction Creek Road) is narrow, making it difficult for cars to pass.

Highlights: This is a traditional Durango ride, with lots of singletrack and a beautiful view of the Junction Creek valley, and it can be done round-trip from town. Described here as a counter-clockwise ride, many people prefer to go clockwise to avoid the tough climb.

Land status: San Juan National Forest; Colorado Division of Wildlife.

Maps: San Juan National Forest; USGS Durango West.

Access: Start from anywhere in town. As described here, odometer readings start at 2nd Avenue West and 25th Street in Durango.

The ride:

0.0 From 2nd Avenue West, go west slightly uphill on 25th Street, which soon becomes Junction Creek Road (County Road 204).

3.5 At a cattleguard the road turns from pavement to gravel. (There is a small parking lot here for those who want to do an out-and-back ride.) Turn left off the road, cross a tiny (usually dry) gully, and pedal onto the Colorado Trail, climbing slightly as it follows Junction Creek. The trail here is mostly smooth, with some rocky sections and very short climbs.

3.8 Cross a tributary of Junction Creek on a small wooden bridge. Continue left (west).

4.8 After a short, steep climb, pass a spur trail on the right coming from Junction Creek Road, just 100 yards away at this point. Continue west on the Colorado Trail and begin a section that is steeper and includes several short, strenuous climbs where the slope drops quickly away from the trail. Use caution.

5.8   Begin a fun downhill section, but watch for a couple of big rocks.

6.3   The trail turns left to cross a bridge over Junction Creek. From here, begin a steep, 1.6-mile climb with several technical switchbacks. (If you're not up for such a long, sweat-inducing climb, this is a good point to turn back.)

7.9   Top out and celebrate at Gudy's Rest. Have some water and a seat overlooking the Junction Creek valley. In the distance you can see the mesa where Fort Lewis College resides. When ready, continue on the Colorado Trail, heading slightly downhill. (An option, again, is to turn back here.)

8.1   Turn left (south) onto the Hoffheins Connection Trail, heading slightly downhill. The tread is generally smooth, with several short, steep, rocky sections. (For a longer loop, go straight here, staying on the Colorado Trail another 2.8 miles. Go left onto Dry Fork Trail,

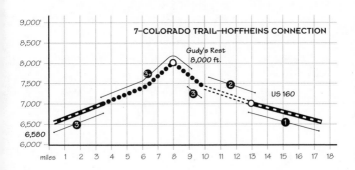

down a fun, twisting, gentle downhill for 3.4 miles. At a three-way junction, veer right onto the Hoffheins Connection Trail. You'll be at the 9.3-mile mark listed below. This longer loop adds 5 miles to the ride. It incorporates Ride 6 in reverse.)

9.3 Veer left at a three-way junction. The Dry Fork Trail is on the right.

9.5 Climb over a stock fence on a set of stairs.

10.2 Reach the end of the singletrack and cross a cattleguard into a small parking lot. Continue on a fairly level dirt road. Once out of the parking lot, turn right (southeast).

11.1 Hit Dry Fork Road. Keep left, heading downhill.

13.1 Reach the paved Lightner Creek Road and go left (south).

14.2 At a junction with U.S. Highway 160 go left and downhill, watching for cars screaming down from the right.

17.6 Reach the intersection of Camino del Rio and US 160 in Durango. (It's another 1.6 miles back to our starting point at 25th Street and 2nd Avenue West, if you choose to go that way.)

Colorado Trail from Sliderock Trail

[See map on page 33]

Location: North and west of Durango in the San Juan National Forest.

Distance: 45.5-mile loop (or 23.6 miles one way if you shuttle to the trailhead).

Time: 5.5 to 8 hours (3 to 5 hours on Colorado Trail portion).

Tread: 7 miles on paved road; 17.6 miles on gravel road, 0.8 mile on dirt road; 20.1 miles on singletrack. (A shuttle to the trailhead leaves 20.1 miles on singletrack and 3.5 miles on paved road to return to town.)

Aerobic level: Strenuous, because of the length and a 1,000-foot climb on the Colorado Trail.

Technical difficulty: 1 on road, 3 and 4 on trail.

Hazards: Bring food and possibly even a water filter for this long ride. Storms can move in surprisingly quickly over the mountains to the west; be prepared.

Highlights: Parts of the Colorado Trail have a back-of-beyond feel, and basically, that's where this section takes you. The singletrack is sweet, thanks to work by trail crews.

Land status: San Juan National Forest.

Maps: San Juan National Forest; USGS Durango West, Monument Hill.

Access: Ride from town. Odometer readings start at 2nd Avenue West and 25th Street. To make this ride easier, drive up the road part way, or all the way, to the trailhead.

The ride:

0.0 Pedal west slightly uphill on 25th Street, which soon becomes Junction Creek Road (County Road 204).

3.5 At a cattleguard the road turns from pavement to gravel. The Colorado Trail starts here on the left, but instead continue pedaling uphill on Junction Creek Road, which starts to get a bit steeper.

5.7 Pass the Log Chutes Trailhead and parking area on the right.

10.6 Pass the Animas Overlook as the road bends to the west.

14.2 Enjoy a downhill section. From here, the road rolls up and down with short sections of rough tread.

21.1 Turn left off of Junction Creek Road onto a spur road going southwest. This rocky, dirt road starts off fairly flat. There should be a sign here pointing toward the Sliderock Trail.

21.9 The Colorado Trail crosses the spur road here. Turn left, heading south and downhill on singletrack. (Right goes up toward Kennebec Pass; see Ride 9.)

25.3 Cross a creek. From here the trail becomes rougher in spots, though still rideable for the most part.

26.7 Cross a nice bridge that seems out of place here in the backwoods. On the south side of Junction Creek, begin a major uphill, extremely steep in places, that climbs 1,000 feet in 4.5 miles.

27.8 Reach a high point but don't be fooled—there is still lots of climbing ahead.

29.1 Begin another gruelling climb.

29.8 Hit a high point. There is still some climbing to do, but it won't be as steep.

31.2 Yes, you have reached the top of the climb! The track gets wider here as it joins an old road.

34.4 Cross a talus rock section and go through a swinging gate.

34.7 Hit the junction of the Colorado Trail and Dry Fork Trail. Veer left (east) on the Colorado Trail, back on true singletrack. The trail climbs briefly, then begins a fun descent with several waterbars.

37.4 Ignore the turnoff for the Hoffheins Connection Trail on the right.

37.6 Reach Gudy's Rest, which is a great place to rest and offers a nice view. But you're probably anxious to finish the ride. Begin a 1.6-mile descent that features several tight switchbacks and a couple of rocky sections. Watch for runners, hikers, and other mountain bikers; this is a *very* busy section of trail.

39.2 End the descent and cross a bridge over Junction Creek.

40.7 A spur trail that veers left here leads to Junction Creek

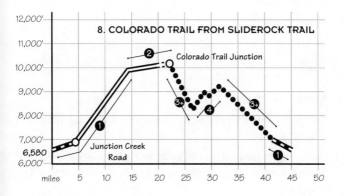

Road in 100 yards. To finish the Colorado Trail, veer right, downhill.

42.0 Come to the end of the trail and turn right onto Junction Creek Road, heading slightly downhill, briefly on gravel, then in 20 yards onto pavement.

45.5 Finish this epic ride at 2nd Avenue West and 25th Street.

Kennebec Pass

Location: Northwest of Durango in the La Plata Mountains, on the San Juan National Forest.

Distance: 49.2-mile loop from town. This ride can be made shorter by driving to Mayday or somewhere else along La Plata Canyon Road.

Time: 5 to 8 hours.

Tread: 18.4 miles on pavement; 25.2 miles on gravel road; 3 miles on four-wheel-drive and rocky dirt road; 2.6 miles on singletrack and doubletrack.

Aerobic level: Strenuous.

Technical difficulty: 2 and 3, with 4+ on the Sliderock Trail for exposure.

Hazards: It's good to ride this one on a really clear day because Kennebec Pass can get very cold and nasty during a storm. Use

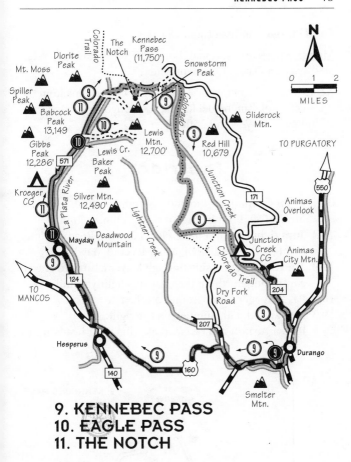

9. KENNEBEC PASS
10. EAGLE PASS
11. THE NOTCH

caution on the Sliderock Trail—the talus near the top is difficult to ride and the potential fall from there would be spectacular.

Highlights: This is the classic long-distance, high-altitude Durango ride. If you say, "I rode Kennebec yesterday," people may not be in awe, but they surely will respect you.

Land status: San Juan National Forest.

Maps: San Juan National Forest; USGS Durango West, Hesperus, La Plata, Monument Hill.

Access: Begin from town. The mileage below begins from the intersection of Camino del Rio and U.S. Highway 160. It ends at 2nd Avenue West and 25th Street.

The ride:

0.0 From Camino del Rio and US 160, go uphill and west on US 160. From here you climb, climb, climb.

10.4 Turn right (north) onto La Plata Canyon Road (County Road 124). The grade is fairly level to Mayday.

14.9 The road, after passing through Mayday, turns to gravel, continuing north up the canyon, slightly uphill.

16.5 Pass Kroeger Campground on the left.

19.3 Pass an old, tall chimney on the right.

19.6 Pass a turnoff at Lewis Creek; this road heads up to

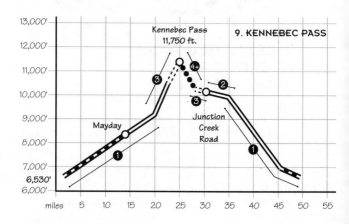

Eagle Pass (see Ride 10). Continue up La Plata Canyon as the road gets steeper and more rugged.

22.5 Veer left (north) on Kennebec Pass Road (Forest Road 571) where it joins Columbus Basin Road (FR 498). You're now on four-wheel-drive road.

23.2 Cross the headwaters of the La Plata River at a switchback, momentarily heading south. This marks the beginning of a steep, uphill, technical section.

24.1 The grade slacks off as you reach an open area at timberline.

24.2 At an old boiler tank (part of the old Cumberland Mine), veer left down a short hill, then climb again up a smooth grade.

24.7 Top out on a wide ridge. To the left (west) is the Highline Trail, which doubles as the Colorado Trail here. Instead, go right (southeast) for 20 yards, where a singletrack tread (also the Colorado Trail) goes left (east) toward Kennebec Pass. (The road continues toward The Notch—see Ride 11.)

25.3 After one more big climb, arrive at Kennebec Pass and enjoy the views east and north. The route follows an old road here.

25.4 Take a left off the old road and go northeast on singletrack, the Sliderock Trail. This section is very tricky because it's steep, technical, and has a scary dropoff on the right. The talus sections are very loose; please get off your bike unless you're an extremely experienced rider.

27.3 Come to a spur road off Junction Creek Road. Go left (northeast) and downhill on the road. (Actually, you have a choice to return to town via the Colorado Trail, which crosses the road here. Keep in mind that it will take 1 to 2 hours longer on the trail, and there's a 1,000-foot climb. See the description for Ride 8, mile 21.9.)

28.1 Come to Junction Creek Road (FR 171) and go right (east). Thought you'd gained a lot of elevation? Well, for most of the first 3 miles on Junction Creek Road you will climb some more. Nothing extremely steep, however.

35.0 Top out on the last minor climb. Now it's all fast downhill. Watch for cars.

38.6 Pass the Animas Overlook and bank into a switchback, now heading west.

45.7 The road goes from gravel to pavement and becomes CR 204. On the right is the Colorado Trail trailhead. Continue slightly downhill on the pavement.

49.2 Reach the intersection of 2nd Avenue West and 25th Street. Find your way home.

Eagle Pass
[See map on page 43]

Location: Northwest of Durango in the La Plata Mountains, on the San Juan National Forest.

Distance: 9 miles out-and-back.

Time: 1.5 to 2.5 hours.

Tread: All steep four-wheel-drive road.

Aerobic level: Strenuous.

Technical difficulty: 3 and 4.

Hazards: This one just keeps getting steeper the higher you go. If you're not in decent shape, this ride could kill you. There aren't any major dropoffs, but be careful on the descent; it's steep and rocky with a few ruts.

Highlights: This is a classic high-altitude training ride. If this doesn't make you hurt, consider going pro. Fields of colorful wildflowers treat riders who make this trek.

Land status: San Juan National Forest. At press time, ownership of this road was in doubt. Before riding here, call the Columbine Ranger District (see Appendix B) and ask about any travel restrictions.

Maps: San Juan National Forest; USGS La Plata.

Access: From the intersection of Camino del Rio and U.S. Highway 160 in Durango, go west 10.4 miles on US 160 to County Road 124 (La Plata Canyon Road). Take CR 124 north 9.2 miles to Lewis Creek and Eagle Pass Road (0.3 mile past the chimney on the right side of the road). Turn off the road and park.

The ride:

0.0   Go east, starting out with a short downhill. Don't get used to it. Cross a bridge over the La Plata River and start the climb.

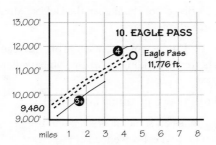

1.3 Cross a small stream as the road continues to get steeper and more technical.

1.9 Cross another small stream.

3.1 Come to an old mine and a Y junction. Go right (north) and uphill, passing through a gate. Please obey private property signs, if there are any.

4.4 The road tops out and begins a slight descent.

4.5 Come to a bend in the road at the ridge line. The road bends from southeast to northeast and begins a steep descent here. Stop here and enjoy the view east toward Durango, south toward Silver Mountain, and west across the valley. To the north is Lewis Mountain. When you're done admiring the view, return the way you came—but first make sure your brakes work.

9.0 Back at the parking area.

The Notch

[See map on page 43]

Location: Northwest of Durango in the La Plata Mountains, on the San Juan National Forest.

Distance: 21.4 miles out-and-back. This ride can be made longer or shorter, depending on where you park along La Plata Canyon Road.

Time: 2.5 to 4 hours, if starting from Mayday.

Tread: 15.2 miles on sometimes steep and rough gravel road, 6.2 miles on four-wheel-drive road.

Aerobic level: Strenuous.

Technical difficulty: A mix of 2, 3, and 4.

Hazards: Beware the high altitude. The air can get thin and the weather turns nasty in a hurry.

Highlights: From The Notch there are spectacular views east toward Durango and north and west toward mountains. This is a good high-altitude training ride.

Land status: San Juan National Forest.

Maps: San Juan National Forest; USGS La Plata.

Access: From the intersection of Camino del Rio and U.S. Highway 160 in Durango, go west 10.4 miles on US 160 to County Road 124 (La Plata Canyon Road). Take CR 124 north 4.5 miles just past the town of Mayday to a large parking area. Here, the paved road turns to gravel.

The ride:

0.0   Go north on the gravel road, slightly uphill.
1.6   Pass Kroeger Campground on the left.
4.4   Pass an old, tall chimney on the right.

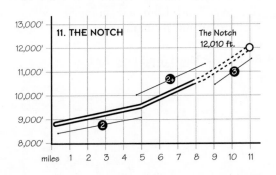

4.7   Pass a turnoff at Lewis Creek; this road heads up to Eagle Pass (see Ride 10). Continue up La Plata Canyon as the road gets steeper and more rugged.

7.6   Veer left (north) on Kennebec Pass Road (Forest Road 571) where it joins Columbus Basin Road (FR 498). You're now on four-wheel-drive road.

8.3   Cross the headwaters of the La Plata River at a switchback, momentarily heading south. This marks the beginning of a steep, uphill, technical section.

9.2   The road grade slacks off as it reaches an open area at timberline. Look for The Notch up to the right (southeast).

9.3   At an old boiler tank, part of the old Cumberland Mine, veer left down a short hill, then climb again up a smooth grade.

9.8   Top out on a wide ridge. To the left (west) is the Highline Trail, which doubles as the Colorado Trail here. Instead, continue right (southeast) along the ridge toward The Notch. In 20 yards, the Colorado Trail splits left toward Kennebec Pass (see Ride 9.)

10.7   Go through The Notch, but not more than a few feet. You'll see why. If the weather is decent, this is a great place for lunch. You can see Durango toward the southeast, with Junction Creek below you. The road actually continues south from here, going below Snowstorm Peak, but is not recommended. Return the way you came.

21.4   Back at the Mayday parking area.

Old Railroad Grade

Location: 20 miles west of Durango in the foothills of the La Plata Mountains, in the San Juan National Forest.

Distance: 6.4 miles one way (12.8-mile out-and-back) or 13.8-mile round trip.

Time: 1.5 to 2 hours for out-and-back.

Tread: All dirt road for out-and-back; 8.3 miles on dirt and 5.5 miles on paved highway for round trip.

Aerobic level: Easy.

Technical difficulty: 1.

Hazards: No major worries, but, as always, watch for vehicles.

Highlights: Good early season ride because of low elevation. It's also good for beginning mountain bikers.

Land status: San Juan National Forest.

Maps: San Juan National Forest; USGS Thompson Park.

Access: From Durango drive 20 miles west on U.S. Highway 160 to the turnoff for the Madden Peak Road

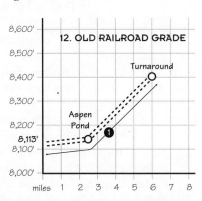

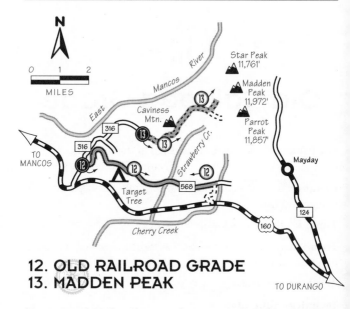

12. OLD RAILROAD GRADE
13. MADDEN PEAK

(Forest Road 316) at the top of Mancos Hill. Drive 0.9 mile to the turnoff for FR 568 and park.

The ride:

0.0   Begin a level ride east on a dirt road, a former railroad grade.
1.0   The road heads north. Pass tiny ponds on the north side of the road, then turn back east.
2.4   Pass Aspen Pond.
6.4   Come to a junction. The road going right drops off steeply from the railroad grade. This is the suggested place to turn back, although you can keep going. (To make the round trip, take this steep dirt road 1 mile to US 160, turn right and pedal 5.5 miles west to Madden Peak Road and 0.9 mile back to your car.)

Madden Peak

Location: In the west La Plata Mountains, San Juan National Forest.

Distance: 11.2 miles out and back, not including a hike to the top.

Time: 2 to 4 hours, not including hike.

Tread: 1.2 miles on gravel road; 6.6 miles on dirt road; 3.4 miles on four-wheel-drive road.

Aerobic level: Strenuous.

Technical difficulty: Mostly 2, some 4.

Hazards: Coming down, watch for ruts and rocks. On the hike to the top, be wary of cleats slipping on rock.

Highlights: Some great views toward the west and a great way to see the southern La Platas. The hike up Madden Peak is well worthwhile. (Consider packing a lock for your bike.)

Land status: San Juan National Forest.

Maps: San Juan National Forest; USGS Thompson Park, Rampart Hills, Hesperus and La Plata.

Access: From Durango drive west 20 miles on U.S. Highway 160, then go right onto Madden Peak Road (Forest Road 316) on top of Mancos Hill. You can park here, or drive as far as 8.1 miles. To follow this guide, drive 4.1 miles and park just before a retention pond on the south side of the road. This allows you to get a decent warmup before the steep stuff.

The ride:

0.0   Start east and uphill on a good gravel road.

0.6   The road becomes less well-maintained and rougher, but still offers a good riding surface.

1.9   Veer left at a Y at Valley View Springs.

2.7   A road left (FR 353) goes up to radio towers on Caviness Mountain. Continue straight (east), coming to a short downhill section.

4.0   Veer right at a Y in an area of recent heavy logging. A swinging metal gate is open from June 15 to September 31.

4.2   At another junction veer right for a more mellow (but still steep) road, which soon makes a left-hand switchback.

4.5   The forks from mile 4.2 rejoin.

4.9   Go right at this junction, unless you're an incredible climber. You can later return via the steeper road on the left.

5.1   Come to a clearing and a junction. Go left up a steep, rocky section. This is rideable if you still have enough energy and pick a good line. Before doing so, admire the views west of Mancos, Mesa Verde, Sleeping Ute Mountain, and the Abajo Mountains in Utah way off in the distance.

5.7   End of the line for the road. Stash your bike behind a tree and hike northeast and east, following the

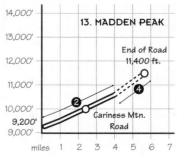

ridge, to the top of Madden Peak, a gain of about 500 feet in elevation. Up and back takes about an hour. The ride back is fast, and by going down the steeper way, you save about 0.2 mile on the return.

7.2   Back at seasonal closure gate (mile 4.0).

11.2   Return to car.

North Fork West Mancos Loop

Location: In the west La Plata Mountains, San Juan National Forest.

Distance: 15.1-mile loop.

Time: 2.5 to 4 hours.

Tread: 1.5 miles on gravel road; 4.4 miles on abandoned road; 3.1 miles on dirt road; 6.1 miles on singletrack.

Aerobic level: Moderate to strenuous.

Technical difficulty: 3 with some 4.

Hazards: This is a fairly remote area with lots of trails. Let someone know where you're going.

Highlights: Beautiful, fun, little-used trails with some nice singletrack.

Land status: San Juan National Forest.

Maps: San Juan National Forest; USGS Rampart Hills and La Plata.

14. NORTH FORK WEST MANCOS LOOP
15. BURNT RIDGE LOOP
16. BIG WEST MANCOS LOOP

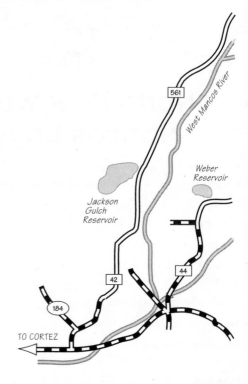

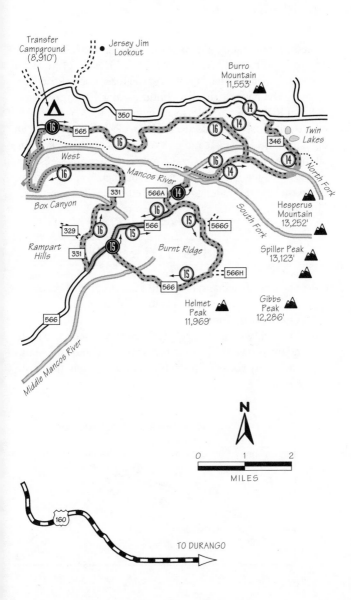

Access: From Durango drive 24 miles west on U.S. Highway 160 to Echo Basin Road (County Road 44). Go 2.4 miles on pavement, then go straight onto a gravel road, Forest Road 566, ignoring the paved road that continues at a 90-degree angle. Follow FR 566 for 5.4 miles to a Y intersection. (Make sure you go past the first Y intersection, where FR 331 goes left in an open meadow.) Veer left and go another 1.8 miles to FR 566A, taking another left there. Go 0.7 mile and park at a forest service gate, which is open during the summer. You could drive down the first 0.8 mile of this ride, but it doesn't seem necessary.

The ride:

0.0 Start northeast and downhill on a rough dirt road.
0.7 Veer right where the roads fork, following a sign to the Owen Basin Trailhead.
0.8 Veer left where the roads fork, continuing downhill. In about 100 yards the road becomes a trail and almost immediately goes down steeply to ford a stream, the South

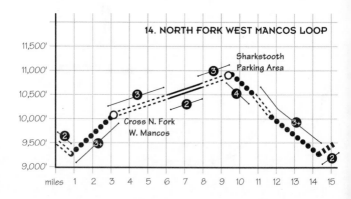

Fork of the West Mancos River. Ride up from the stream and come to an open meadow, following brown wooden poles.

1.0 Come to a junction and go right (east). This is the West Mancos Trail, although the current sign does not say so.

1.1 At another trail junction, turn left (east) up a set of switchbacks, staying on the West Mancos Trail. The tread is steep but not too technical and mostly rideable. The trail to the right is the Owen Basin Trail.

2.0 Cross a small stream to Horse Fly Flats. Look for a series of brown wooden poles and follow them and a faint trail to the northeast. Enter a series of ups and downs with a couple of tiny creek crossings.

3.1 Join an old road grade and enjoy views up ahead (east) of Sharkstooth, Centennial, and Hesperus mountains.

3.3 Come to a junction that may not look like one. The old road makes a switchback to the right (southwest), but go left (north-northwest) downhill. Go 50 yards to the North Fork of the West Mancos. On the other side is an obvious track—another old road grade. Be careful fording the stream and negotiating the steep banks on either side, and head for the old road grade on the other side, going northwest.

4.7 Join the Aspen Loop (an ATV route in this area) and veer left (west), continuing on the road you've been on. Another part of the Aspen Loop goes right uphill (north), but ignore it.

5.1 Pass a pond on the left, with Helmet Peak in the distance.

5.4 At an intersection, take a 120-degree right (northeast) uphill on another old road grade.

6.2 Come to FR 350, a well-graded gravel road, and go right (east), continuing to climb.

7.7 Turn right onto FR 346 toward Twin Lakes and Sharkstooth Trailhead on a rough dirt road, climbing gradually.

8.4 Pass Twin Lakes on the left.

9.2 Come to the Sharkstooth Trailhead and a small parking lot. Instead of taking Sharkstooth Trail, turn right (south) onto a rough dirt road heading slightly uphill. This is the West Mancos Trail.

9.4 The tread becomes singletrack and begins to drop. This section is tricky, with tree roots and rocks.

9.9 Cross the North Fork of the West Mancos on a set of logs. Look up at the strange horizontal stripes on Hesperus Mountain. After the crossing, the trail turns southwest and climbs briefly. Be careful not to lose the trail here as it continues mostly downhill through some rough, rooted sections.

10.9 Join an old road grade. The track is very faint in places; follow West Mancos Trail signs.

11.8 Come to the 3.3-mile junction and return the way you came, going west and slightly downhill, hitting true singletrack in 0.2 mile.

13.1 Return to Horse Fly Flats and begin a fun downhill stretch.

14.0 Hit the junction with Owen Basin Trail. Go right.

14.1 Head left at the T and follow poles to the South Fork of the West Mancos.

14.3 Cross the stream and head uphill on FR 566A.

15.1 Loop complete.

Burnt Ridge Loop

[See map on page 57]

Location: In the west La Plata Mountains, San Juan National Forest.

Distance: 8.7-mile loop.

Time: 1 to 1.5 hours.

Tread: All gravel and dirt road.

Aerobic level: Easy to moderate.

Technical difficulty: 2+.

Hazards: Watch for occasional vehicles on the narrow road.

Highlights: Nice way to see the La Platas without straining too much.

Land status: San Juan National Forest.

Maps: San Juan National Forest; USGS Rampart Hills.

Access: From Durango drive 24 miles west on U.S. Highway 160 to Echo Basin Road (County Road 44). Go 2.4 miles on pavement, then go straight onto a gravel road, Forest Road 566, ignoring the paved road that continues at a 90-degree angle. Follow FR 566 for 5.4 miles to a Y intersection. These are your starting and finishing routes, the legs of FR 566 as it begins and ends a loop. Find a place to park.

The ride:

0.0 At the Y, veer left (north) up a good grade on a gravel road.

0.8 After a downhill, cross a cattleguard with a large boulder field on the right.

1.8 The turnoff for Owen Basin Trailhead (see Ride 14) is on the left. Continue straight on FR 566 as the road becomes dirt and gets rockier.

2.9 Top out after a steady climb and enjoy views of Hesperus Mountain to the east and several other peaks in the La Platas.

3.5 FR 566G goes left (northwest) here. Continue west on FR 566.

4.5 FR 566N goes left (southeast). Continue south toward Helmet Peak.

5.5 Climb a short rise to a T intersection. Go right (west), staying on FR 566.

5.8 Hit the high point of the trip at a pass, and begin downhill heading southwest.

6.5 Ignore the spur road on the left. Continue right (southwest).

7.3 Enjoy views of the Mancos Valley and Sleeping Ute Mountain beyond Jackson Reservoir.

8.7 Return to the starting point at the Y intersection.

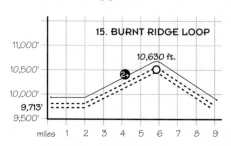

Big West Mancos Loop

[See map on page 57]

Location: In the west La Plata Mountains circling around the West Mancos River canyon, in the San Juan National Forest.

Distance: 24.1-mile loop.

Time: 3.5 to 6 hours.

Tread: 1.8 miles on smooth gravel road; 16.8 miles on dirt road, which can sometimes be smooth, sometimes rough; 0.5 mile on rough abandoned road; 5 miles on singletrack.

Aerobic level: Strenuous due to length and a climb near the end.

Technical difficulty: From 1 to 5.

Hazards: Some of this track is fairly remote. Have a good map, someone who knows how to read it, lots of food, and raingear.

Highlights: Riders experience all types of tread on this big loop, and circle around a huge section of the West Mancos River, dropping in and out of it twice.

Land status: San Juan National Forest.

Maps: San Juan National Forest; USGS Rampart Hills and La Plata.

Access: From Durango drive 28 miles west on U.S. Highway 160 to Mancos. Turn right on Colorado Highway 184, going 0.3 mile to Jackson Gulch Reservoir Road (Forest Road 561). Follow FR 561 for 9 miles and turn right on the Transfer Campground road. Go about 0.2 mile and park near the campground.

The ride:

0.0 Take the road that leads northwest past the campground.

0.5 Veer left (to the right is a parking area). In 100 yards it's the end of the line for motor vehicles. Continue riding on the smooth, old road grade, climbing steadily.

3.5 A faded road goes right. Stay on the main track.

3.9 A trail on the left heads toward Jersey Jim lookout tower. Continue on the road around a switchback.

5.5 Reach a Y and the Aspen Loop, an ATV path in this area. Veer right (east), going a short way uphill and then heading downhill. The road left connects with FR 350 (see Ride 14).

5.8 Pass a small pond on the right, with a view beyond of Helmet Peak.

6.2 Come to a junction of the Aspen Loop, which takes off left (north). Continue straight (east) on the dirt road.

7.6 Dismount and drop down a steep embankment to cross

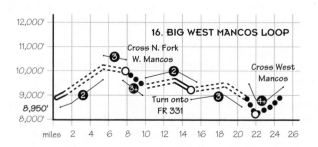

the North Fork of the West Mancos. You might get your feet wet. Continue on a faint track, veering slightly to the right, for about 50 yards. It meets an abandoned road at a switchback; this is the West Mancos Trail. Go right (west) and downhill, hitting singletrack in 0.2 mile.

8.9 Come to Horse Fly Flats, cross a small stream, and take an immediate right. Begin a fun downhill stretch.

9.8 Go right at the junction with the Owen Basin Trail.

9.9 Head left (south) at a T intersection and follow brown wooden poles to the South Fork of the West Mancos.

10.1 Cross the stream and head uphill on dirt FR 566A.

11.6 Turn right (south) onto gravel FR 566, heading downhill.

13.4 Pass a Y intersection, which is the beginning and end of the Burnt Ridge Loop (Ride 15). From here, a fast downhill cruise drops to the next junction.

14.7 Turn right (north) onto FR 331.

15.4 Veer right, continuing on FR 331. (The road left is FR 329.) Overall, FR 331 climbs slightly for the next 3.1 miles.

17.3 Go through a metal gate.

18.5 The road starts a long descent.

21.1 The road pitters out and the track becomes singletrack. It begins to drop steeply down a loose, rocky section that may require you to dismount.

21.7 Come to a junction at the end of the steep descent. Go right (north) along the West Mancos River.

21.8 Cross the West Mancos at a spot that looks good. There may be a makeshift log bridge, or you may have to ford. Find an abandoned road on the other side and go right, continuing north. This is the West Mancos Trail.

21.9 Come to the Box Canyon Trail. Continue straight on

the West Mancos Trail. The going gets a little rough and demands some bike-pushing and carrying. (It is a little easier, however, to turn left onto the Box Canyon Trail, which runs back up to FR 561 and avoids some, but not all, of the bike-pushing to come.)

22.1   The track becomes singletrack.

23.4   The trail starts a steep climb, and goes well above the river. Most of this section is rideable.

23.8   At a junction, go left (northwest) on the Transfer Trail, continuing uphill. (If you go right here you continue on the West Mancos Trail for about 10 difficult miles and eventually land back at mile 9.9 of this ride. This is not recommended.)

24.1   End the difficult climb and hit the road leading to the campground. Go right a short distance to your vehicle.

Chicken Creek

Location: Following cross-country ski loops west of the La Plata Mountains, in the San Juan National Forest.

Distance: 9.5-mile out-and-back with two loops that make a figure eight.

Time: 1 to 2 hours.

Tread: 7.7 miles on dirt road; 1.8 miles on gravel road.

Aerobic level: Easy.

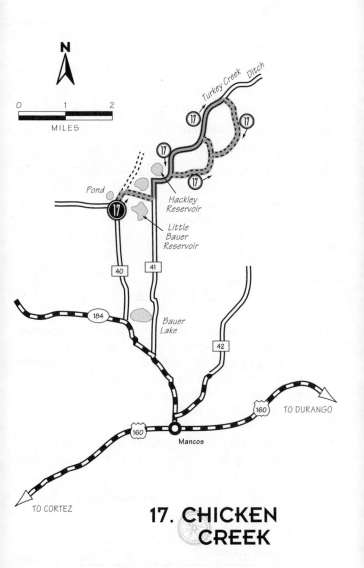

17. CHICKEN CREEK

Technical difficulty: 2.

Hazards: Watch for cars, mainly on the gravel road, but they can be anywhere on this route.

Highlights: A nice mellow ride in a ponderosa forest.

Land status: San Juan National Forest.

Maps: San Juan National Forest; USGS Millwood.

Access: From Durango drive 28 miles on U.S. Highway 160 west to Mancos. Turn right on Colorado Highway 184, going 2.6 miles to County Road 40. (Don't turn on Chicken Creek Road, CR 41. Instead, follow signs to Chicken Creek Cross-country Ski Area.) Go 2.6 miles on CR 40 to the cross-country ski area parking lot.

The ride:

0.0 From the parking area, which is next to a reservoir with dead tree stumps, pedal northeast on Forest Road 390, a flat, fairly smooth dirt road. You are following the Little Bauer Loop of the cross-country ski area.

0.2 Where the roads diverge, go right (east), crossing a tiny stream which may be dry.

0.4 Veer left at a Y.

0.9 Continue past a turnoff that goes right (south) to Little Bauer Reservoir.

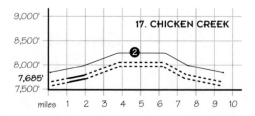

1.1 Come to a swinging gate and, a few feet beyond, Chicken Creek Road. Go left (north) up the gravel road.

1.6 The road makes a 90-degree turn right (east).

2.0 Just after a cattleguard, take the Dolph Kuss Loop going right (east) off the gravel road. The Kuss dirt road tends uphill and is rough in spots, but it is easy to negotiate. Follow the blue diamond markers on the trees if in question.

2.1 Veer left at a Y junction.

2.3 Veer right at a Y junction.

3.5 Meet up with the end of the Hamlin Loop, coming in from the right. Continue straight (north) on the Kuss Loop.

3.8 Come to Chicken Creek Road and go right (northeast) up a slight grade. You are now on the Hamlin Loop.

4.4 Make a right off the main road, following a sign to Chicken Creek Canyon Overlook. The trail bends around to go southeast.

4.7 Just after a metal gate (probably open) veer left, continuing to follow the blue diamonds.

5.9 Meet up with the Kuss Loop (at mile 3.5 above). Continue north.

6.2 Hit Chicken Creek Road and go left (southwest) and downhill. The road is fast until just past the cattleguard. Be mindful of ruts and cars.

7.5 Pass the turn to the Kuss Loop (at mile 2.0 above). From here, retrace your route to the parking lot.

8.4 Turn off Chicken Creek Road and go back through the swinging gate (mile 1.1).

9.5 Enter the parking lot.

Hermosa Creek

Location: North of Durango between Purgatory Ski Resort and the town of Hermosa. Follows Hermosa Creek.

Distance: 19.6 miles point to point.

Time: 2 to 4 hours

Tread: 5.1 miles on doubletrack; 14.5 miles on singletrack.

Aerobic level: Moderate, although a 1.2-mile climb near the end can be a killer.

Technical difficulty: Mostly 3, with some 3+ and 4.

Hazards: The trail sometimes contours along steep valley sides, with sheer dropoffs. Watch for other riders, hikers, horseback riders, cattle, and motorcycles—it's open to all.

Highlights: Great singletrack riding in a beautiful valley. Plus, it's mostly downhill. Another classic Durango-area ride.

Land status: San Juan National Forest.

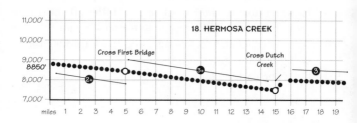

Maps: San Juan National Forest; USGS Hermosa Peak, Elk Creek, Monument Hill, Hermosa.

Access: This ride involves a shuttle, with cars parked on either end. From Durango, drive 10 miles north on U.S. Highway 550, just past Hermosa, and turn left on County Road 203. Go only 30 yards and turn right onto CR 201. Drive 4.2 miles to road's end, the south Hermosa Creek Trailhead.

With the second car, retrace your path back to US 550 and continue north 16 miles to Purgatory Resort. Turn left (west) toward the ski area, but in 0.4 mile turn away from the resort village and onto Forest Road 578. Drive 8.4 miles and turn left (south) on a road that crosses East Fork of Hermosa Creek and ends at the north Hermosa Creek Trailhead.

To make the shuttle shorter, park on the south end near the junction of CR 203 and 201. There is room for a couple of cars at a pullout next to the train tracks on CR 201. Park the second vehicle on the north end 3 miles up FR 578, before dropping into the East Fork Hermosa Creek valley. The extra distance on the bike saddle for this option is all downhill.

The ride:

0.0 Begin from the north Hermosa Creek Trailhead, riding on a wide path on the left (east) side of Hermosa Creek.

2.0 Pass the East Cross Creek Trail on the left.

5.1 Cross the first of two bridges. At this point, the wide track becomes singletrack.

6.1 Cross the second bridge, back to the left (east) side of Hermosa Creek.

10.7 Go around a bend and over a cattle guard. Then begins an excellent singletrack section that contours in and out of several minor drainages.

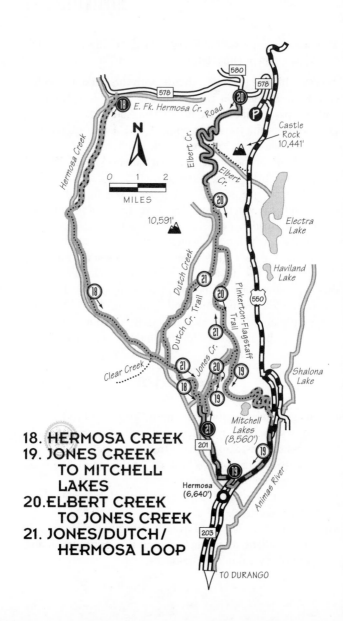

580

578

578

578

E. Fk. Hermosa Cr. Road

18

20

P

Castle
Rock
10,441'

N

Hermosa Creek

Elbert Cr.

Elbert
Cr.

0   1   2
MILES

10,591'

Electra
Lake

Haviland
Lake

18

Dutch Creek

Dutch Cr. Trail

20

21

21

20

550

Pinkerton-Flagstaff Trail

21

Clear Creek

21

Jones Cr.

18

20

21

20

19

19

19

Shalona
Lake

Mitchell
Lakes
(8,560')

18. HERMOSA CREEK
19. JONES CREEK
    TO MITCHELL
    LAKES
20. ELBERT CREEK
    TO JONES CREEK
21. JONES/DUTCH/
    HERMOSA LOOP

201

21

19

19

Hermosa
(6,640')

Animas River

203

TO DURANGO

14.8 Cross Dutch Creek on a wooden bridge and begin a 500-foot, 1.2-mile ascent. If you're bonking, this stretch can be character building (brutal).

16.0 Reach the top of the most difficult part of the climb. The trail climbs again, but only for short stretches.

19.5 Veer left at a Y junction.

19.6 Veer left again at another Y junction, and climb a short, steep section up to CR 201, the south end of Hermosa Creek Trail.

Jones Creek to Mitchell Lakes

Location: 10 miles north of Durango, above Hermosa Creek and down into the Animas River valley, in the San Juan National Forest.

Distance: 18.5-mile loop.

Time: 2.5 to 4 hours

Tread: 2 miles on smooth gravel road; 6.9 miles on singletrack; 1.2 miles on steep, wide singletrack; 2.8 miles on loose, steep dirt road; 5.6 miles on pavement.

Aerobic level: Strenuous, with a 2,700-foot climb, and plenty of up and down on the ridge.

Technical difficulty: A lot of 3; some 4 and 4+ on the steep dirt road.

Hazards: Steep descent on road with loose dirt. If it's really dry, hard braking can fishtail a bike like it is on ice.

Highlights: Nice, continual-grade climb on Jones Creek Trail. Great views from the ridge. Good bike-handlers will enjoy the descent.

Land status: San Juan National Forest.

Maps: San Juan National Forest; USGS Hermosa.

Access: From Durango drive 10 miles north on U.S. Highway 550, just past Hermosa, and turn left on County Road 203. Go only 30 yards to a T intersection and turn right onto County Road 201. Go 0.1 mile and park. There's space for two or three cars on the right next to the train tracks.

The ride:

0.0   Pedal north up CR 201, climbing a consistent grade on pavement.

1.7   The sign says the pavement ends, but it really doesn't.

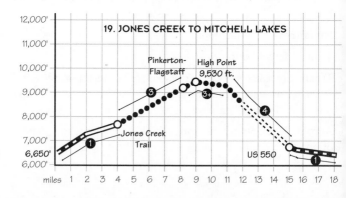

2.0   The pavement ends, but the gravel road remains smooth.

4.0   Look for the Jones Creek Trailhead on the right, going southeast. Begin a long singletrack ascent of moderate to steep gradient. It's broken up twice by short down-hills.

6.3   Cross Jones Creek, which is often dry. Continue to climb.

8.3   Enter a clearing surrounded by aspen where the Jones Creek Trail ends. Cross a tiny creekbed (usually dry) and look for a trail ahead and to the right in the trees, the Pinkerton–Flagstaff Trail. Go east on this wide, smooth trail, pumping slightly uphill. (Ride 21 goes left here on the Pinkerton–Flagstaff.)

8.4   Begin a steeper climb.

8.8   The Animas River valley comes into view as you crest the steepest part of the climb.

9.1   Hit the high point on the ridge at 9,530 feet. Views toward the east are excellent—the Needle Mountains and Missionary Ridge. This is a good point to turn around for riders so inclined. The ridge has several ups and downs from here, and the 3.9-mile descent coming soon (at the 10.9-mile mark) gets hairy and demands strong fingers for braking.

10.9   The trail dives in a left hairpin turn off the ridge. Still on the Pinkerton–Flagstaff, go northeast down steep, wide singletrack that follows a descending ridge. Exercise caution—the trail can be fast, with a couple of rocky, technical sections.

12.1   Roll onto a four-wheel-drive road and continue straight (northeast) plunging downhill. (Going right on the road leads to Mitchell Lakes, which are usually more like swamps.)

13.3 A singletrack trail goes right, but stay on the four-wheel-drive road.

14.5 Cross the tracks of the Durango & Silverton Narrow Gauge Railroad. (Look both ways!) Head down a very rocky section.

14.8 Go through a culvert/tunnel under US 550.

14.9 Come to a paved road and go right.

15.0 At a stop sign next to a KOA campground, go right and uphill on CR 250.

15.2 Turn left (south) onto US 550, heading slightly downhill. The highway rolls up and down (more down) for the next 3.3 miles.

18.5 Cross the railroad tracks and take an immediate right for a shortcut back to the small parking area off CR 201.

Elbert Creek
to Jones Creek
[See map on page 72]

Location: North of Durango, beginning near Purgatory Ski Resort and finishing in Hermosa, in the San Juan National Forest.

Distance: 26.6-mile point-to-point ride.

Time: 3 to 5 hours

Tread: 10.9 miles on singletrack; 3.2 miles on dirt road; 11 miles on gravel road; 1.5 miles pavement.

Aerobic level: Strenuous, with a lot of ups and downs.

Technical difficulty: A lot of 3, some 4 and 4+ on the singletrack.

Hazards: Cow patties are inevitable on this ride. Keep your mouth closed.

Highlights: Lots of singletrack. Like the Hermosa Creek ride (see Ride 18), there's a lot of downhill. That's not to say there's *no* uphill.

Land status: San Juan National Forest.

Maps: San Juan National Forest; USGS Engineer Mountain, Electra Lake, Elk Creek, Hermosa.

Access: This ride involves a shuttle, with cars parked on either end. From Durango, drive 10 miles north on U.S. Highway 550, just past Hermosa, and turn left on County Road 203. Go

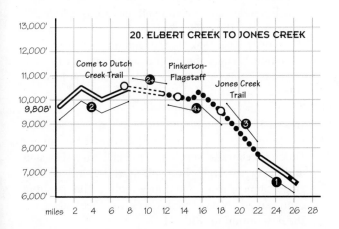

only 30 yards and take a right onto CR 201. Find a place to park; there is usually space next to the railroad tracks.

   With the other car, return to US 550 and continue north 16 miles to Purgatory Resort. Take a left (west) at the ski area's main entrance, but in 0.4 mile turn away from the resort village and onto Forest Road 578. Follow it 3 miles to the junction with Elbert Creek Road (FR 581). Park here.

The ride:

0.0   Go south on Elbert Creek Road (FR 581), heading slightly uphill on this gravel road.

2.0   A road goes left (southeast) to the Hermosa Cliffs overlook. Instead, continue west on the main gravel road, enjoying views to the north of Graysill Mountain and Engineer Mountain.

2.7   Cross a cattleguard at the top of the climb.

5.4   After a left-hand switchback, the road begins to go uphill again. Also at this spot is the Elbert Creek Trail, which goes left and downhill off the road (see Ride 24). Continue on the road, climbing gradually.

8.5   At an open area, look for the Dutch Creek Trail going left (south). There should be a sign on a fence to guide the way. This is basically the high elevation point of the ride, although you will climb some more.

11.7 The road becomes a trail.

13.4 In a small meadow, ignore the faint trail veering left.

13.5 Come to the junction of the Pinkerton–Flagstaff and Dutch Creek trails. Veer left on the Pinkerton–Flagstaff, and begin a stretch of downhills and uphills along a ridge. Some are steep and may require bike-pushing. (You can go out via Dutch Creek also. See mile 9.1 in the description for Ride 21.)

15.1 Pass the Goulding Creek Trail, which goes downhill to the left toward US 550. Resume climbing.

18.3 Turn off the Pinkerton–Flagstaff Trail onto the Jones Creek Trail. This leads right (south) and downhill on fairly smooth singletrack. (Continuing on the Pinkerton–Flagstaff goes to Mitchell Lakes. See Ride 19.)

22.6 Reach a gravel road (FR 576) and turn left (south), downhill.

24.6 The gravel turns to pavement and continues a fast descent. This road is also known as CR 201.

26.6 Arrive back at your car on CR 201.

Jones–Dutch–Hermosa Loop
[See map on page 72]

Location: North of Durango, on a ridge between Hermosa Creek and U.S. Highway 550, in the San Juan National Forest.

Distance: 19.6-mile loop.

Time: 3 to 5.5 hours

Tread: 19.4 miles on singletrack; 0.2 mile on gravel road.

Aerobic level: Strenuous.

Technical difficulty: 4, with some 4+.

Hazards: Cow patties are often abundant. Watch for dropoffs over rocks and roots both on the Pinkerton–Flagstaff and Dutch Creek trails.

Highlights: Lots and lots of singletrack.

Land status: San Juan National Forest.

Maps: San Juan National Forest; USGS Hermosa, Electra Lake, Elk Creek, Monument Hill.

Access: From Durango drive 10 miles north on US 550, just past Hermosa, and turn left on County Road 203. Go only 30 yards and turn right onto CR 201. Drive 4 miles, watching for the Jones Creek trailhead on the right. If you get to the end of the road and the Hermosa Creek Trailhead, double back about 0.1 mile to find Jones Creek Trail.

The ride:

0.0   Pedal east on the Jones Creek Trail up a slight grade. The trails climbs at a similar pace, with two short downhill breaks, until it reaches the ridge.

4.3   In an open area, the Jones Creek Trail disappears. There should be signs here. To the left (northwest), go uphill through an aspen grove on the Pinkerton–Flagstaff

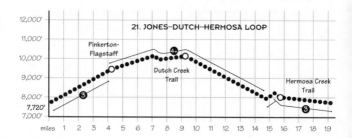

Trail. The Pinkerton–Flagstaff also goes right (east) toward Mitchell Lakes (see Ride 19).

4.5   Begin a steep uphill stretch along the ridge. Some sections likely will require bike-pushing. There's more of the same ahead as the track rolls up and down along the ridge.

7.3   Hit a high point and begin a steep descent down a technical, rooted section of trail.

7.5   Come to a low point and a junction with the Goulding Creek Trail, which drops steeply east through a break in the Hermosa Cliffs. Although it offers a quick emergency bailout to US 550, cyclists should stay off this route. Continue uphill (northeast) on the Pinkerton–Flagstaff.

9.1   Hit the junction with Dutch Creek Trail, which goes left (west) and straight (north). Go left (west) and downhill on a trail that fluctuates between technical/rocky and fast/smooth. The technical sections are sometimes next to steep dropoffs, so be wary.

11.4   Go through or around a wooden stock fence.

14.8   Begin an uphill grunt.

15.2   End this uncalled-for uphill section.

15.6   Come to the Hermosa Creek trail and go left (southeast) up a slight hill. For the next several miles, enjoy a usually smooth, fast track that runs mostly downhill, with a couple of short climbs.

19.3   Veer left at a junction. A right here takes you down to Hermosa Creek and will greatly lengthen your ride.

19.4   Again veer left, going up a short steep hill onto Hermosa Creek Road.

19.6   Arrive at the Jones Creek trailhead and your car.

Old Lime Creek Road

Location: East of U.S. Highway 550 near Coal Bank Pass, in the San Juan National Forest.

Distance: 11.4 miles one way (with shuttle). To make this a longer ride, park at the south junction of US 550 and Old Lime Creek Road; go out-and-back (22.8 miles) or ride up the highway and back on Old Lime Creek Road (19.9 miles).

Time: 1 to 2 hours one-way.

Tread: 11.4 miles on rough dirt road.

Aerobic level: Easy, with one moderate climb.

Technical difficulty: 2+.

Hazards: Watch for automobiles, especially around blind corners. Also watch for other cyclists.

Highlights: This is a fun, scenic ride any time of year, especially in the fall when the aspen are changing. The China Wall is a curiosity.

Land status: San Juan National Forest.

Maps: San Juan National Forest; USGS Engineer Mountain, Snowdon Peak.

Access: From Durango drive 25 miles north on US 550 and continue past Purgatory Ski Resort. Fifty yards after a right-hand switchback and Cascade Creek, turn right onto Old Lime Creek Road and park one vehicle in the huge gravel lot there.

22. OLD LIME CREEK ROAD

In other vehicle, continue up US 550 over Coal Bank Pass; it is 8.5 miles to the north junction with Old Lime Creek Road. Turn right onto Old Lime Creek Road (Forest Road 591) and park.

The ride:

- 0.0 Roll downhill on Old Lime Creek Road, which is fairly bumpy in places but driveable in any passenger vehicle. For the first 1.7 miles the road makes gradual climbs and descents, staying at approximately the same elevation.
- 1.7 The road begins to descend, making switchbacks as it heads for Lime Creek.
- 4.6 Reach creek level at about 9,100 feet. On a really hot day, you can take a quick dip in the freezing water.
- 5.7 Begin a gradual climb up and away from Lime Creek, heading up toward the China Wall, a series of intriguing rock guardrails.
- 7.4 Leave the China Wall and begin a northwest heading, still climbing.
- 7.7 Reach the top of the climb.
- 8.5 Pass a beaver pond on the left. Usually there are birds and animals in the vicinity. Continue the descent.
- 11.4 Return to the parking area.

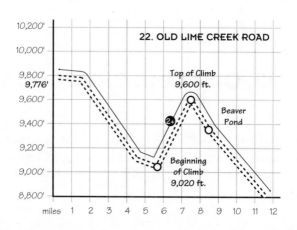

Harris Park Loop

Location: Purgatory Resort, in the San Juan National Forest.

Distance: 3.5-mile loop.

Time: 30 minutes to 1 hour.

Tread: 1.6 miles on gravel road; 1.7 miles on dirt road; 0.2 mile on singletrack (just a taste).

Aerobic level: Easy.

Technical difficulty: 2.

Hazards: Watch for skiers racing down the slopes.

Highlights: This is a fun, easy ride for the whole family. Purgatory marks several routes in its area, including this one, so it shouldn't be hard to follow.

Land status: San Juan National Forest.

Maps: San Juan National Forest; USGS Engineer Mountain.

Access: From Durango drive 25 miles north on U.S. Highway 550 to the Purgatory Resort turnoff. Go left (west) uphill on the paved road, but in 0.4 mile turn away from the resort village and north onto Forest Road 578. Follow it 3 miles to the top of a rise and an intersection with Elbert Creek Road. Park there.

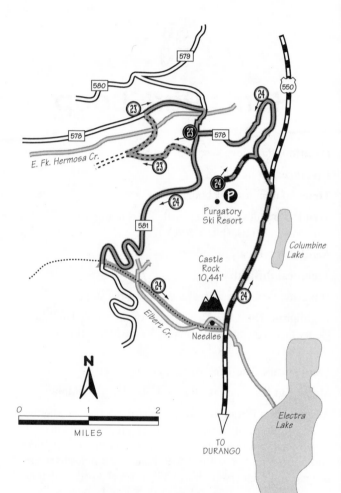

23. HARRIS PARK LOOP
24. ELBERT CREEK LOOP

The ride:

0.0 Go south and slightly uphill on the gravel Elbert Creek Road (FR 581).

0.2 Look for singletrack heading downhill and right (northwest) off the road. Take it, and be careful on the short caprock section.

0.4 Come to a dirt road and turn left (southwest).

0.6 At a four-way intersection, go right (west) and downhill, still on a dirt road.

1.1 Negotiate a switchback.

1.5 Enter the East Fork of Hermosa Creek meadow, near the quad chairlift. Go right (east) and uphill, away from the lift.

1.7 Go through a gate.

2.1 Turn right (east) onto Hermosa Park Road (FR 578), going slightly uphill on the smooth gravel road.

3.1 At the junction of FR 578 and FR 579 (Cascade Divide Road), go right (south), staying on FR 578.

3.5 Back at your starting point. Not enough? Do it again.

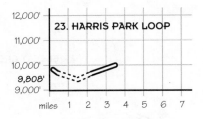

Elbert Creek Loop

[See map on page 86]

Location: South of Purgatory Resort, in the San Juan National Forest.

Distance: 14.8-mile loop.

Time: 1.5 to 3 hours.

Tread: 8.5 miles on gravel road; 3.2 miles on singletrack; 3.1 miles on pavement.

Aerobic level: Moderate.

Technical difficulty: Mostly 2, but some 3 and 4.

Hazards: Some technical, rocky sections on the singletrack. Watch for fast-moving autos on the gravel road.

Highlights: This is a nice half-day loop, excellent when the weather is a bit iffy. Some great views north while climbing Elbert Creek Road.

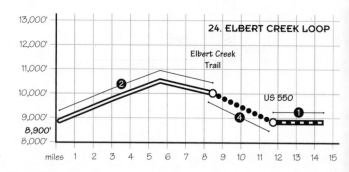

Land status: San Juan National Forest.

Maps: San Juan National Forest; USGS Engineer Mountain, Electra Lake.

Access: From Durango drive 25 miles north on U.S. Highway 550 to the Purgatory Resort turnoff. Go left uphill 0.4 mile on the paved road into the gravel ski area parking lot.

The ride:

- 0.0 Pedal north away from the ski area and onto Hermosa Park Road (Forest Road 578), a gravel road heading slightly uphill. This road gets steeper as it eventually heads west.
- 3.1 Hit the junction of Elbert Creek Road (FR 581) and Hermosa Park Road. Go left (south) on FR 581, heading slightly uphill on this gravel road.
- 4.5 Make a right-hand switchback just before coming to a large building (the Powderhouse at Purgatory).
- 5.1 A road goes left (southeast) to the Hermosa Cliffs overlook. Instead, continue west on the main gravel road, enjoying views to the north of Graysill and Engineer mountains.
- 5.4 Pass under the quad chairlift.
- 5.8 Cross a cattleguard at the top of the climb.
- 8.5 A few yards after a left-hand switchback, watch for an obvious singletrack (possibly unmarked) heading downhill left off the road. Note that from here, the road starts uphill (see Ride 20.) The trail is sometimes rutted and filled with cow pies. It's not very steep, however.
- 9.1 Cross Elbert Creek. The trail grows more technical.
- 9.4 Go through a fence; from here the track becomes steeper and more technical.

9.9 Pass a cabin (still in use) on the right. You're in the trees now, and the trail winds down through a series of fun switchbacks and a couple of rocky sections.
11.7 Go through a gate at the village of Needles and turn left (north) onto US 550.
14.4 Turn left at the Purgatory Resort entrance.
14.8 End your journey at the car.

Cascade Loop

Location: North of Purgatory Ski Resort in the Cascade Creek drainage, in the San Juan National Forest.

Distance: 22.1-mile loop.

Time: 2.5 to 4 hours.

Tread: 9 miles on gravel road; 6.8 miles on rough dirt road; 0.2 mile on faint, abandoned road; 4.2 miles on singletrack; 1.9 miles on pavement.

Aerobic level: Moderate.

Technical difficulty: Mostly 2, but on the singletrack some 3, 4, and even a short section of 5.

Hazards: The drop from Cascade Divide Road to Cascade Creek is tricky. Most riders have to walk parts. Cascade Creek must be forded, but most of the year this is not too difficult.

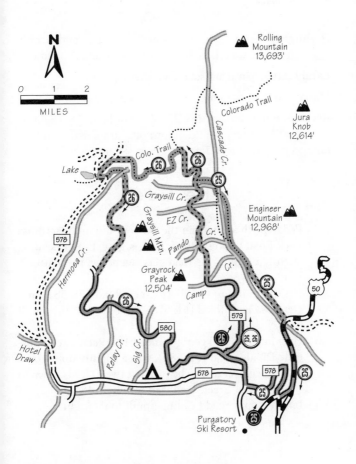

25. CASCADE LOOP
26. CASCADE DIVIDE
TO RELAY CREEK

Highlights: Great views of Engineer Mountain and Grizzly Peak, and some waterfalls on Cascade Creek and tributaries.

Land status: San Juan National Forest.

Maps: San Juan National Forest; USGS Engineer Mountain.

Access: From Durango drive 25 miles north on U.S. Highway 550 to the Purgatory Ski Resort turnoff. Go left and uphill 0.4 mile on the paved road into the gravel ski area parking lot.

The ride:

- 0.0 Pedal north away from the ski area and onto Hermosa Park Road (Forest Road 578), a gravel road heading slightly uphill. This road gets steeper as it eventually heads west.
- 3.1 Hit the junction of Elbert Creek Road (FR 581) and Hermosa Park Road (FR 578). Go right (north) on FR 578.
- 3.6 Hit a junction and go right (north) on Relay Creek/Cascade Divide Road (FR 580), going slightly uphill on a one-lane gravel road. The road left (west) leads down to the Hermosa Creek Trailhead (see Ride 18).
- 3.9 Ignore a spur road heading uphill to the right.

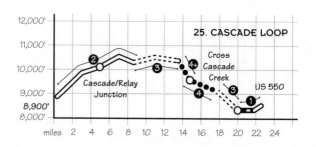

4.9   Go right on Cascade Divide Road (FR 579) where it splits from Relay Creek Road (FR 580). FR 579 goes north then east around a bend, still climbing. (This is the starting point of Ride 26.)

6.7   The road begins to descend with views of Engineer Mountain straight ahead and the Twilight Peaks to the east. For the next 6.8 miles, the road makes short descents and climbs as it contours along and under Graysill Mountain.

8.7   End the downhill. From here the road gets a little rougher but is still easily rideable.

12.0 Cross EZ Creek, usually very easy to do.

13.4 Cross Graysill Creek and go up a fairly steep hill.

13.5 When the road begins to bend left after the Graysill Creek crossing, look for a faint road, no longer in use, taking off slightly downhill to the right (north-northeast). This leads to the Graysill Trail. (If you miss this unmarked road, you will come across the trail 0.2 mile farther on FR 579. The trail is rocky and pretty much unrideable at that point. It is the same one you pick up at the 13.7-mile mark below.)

13.6 Veer left.

13.7 Watch for a trail crossing the abandoned road you're on. Take this trail downhill to the right (east). It is not maintained, and you will almost certainly encounter downfall. It is steep and rocky and rooted in places—a technical challenge.

14.7 As the trail levels out it comes to a Y intersection. You can go either way, but the best seems to be left toward Cascade Creek.

14.8 Ford Cascade Creek and pick up an obvious trail on the other side in an open meadow. Go right (southeast) on the trail, which alternates between smooth and rocky, offering several challenging sections along with fun fast places. This is a fairly popular hiking and horseriding trail. Grizzly Peak is almost due north.

15.4 Engine Creek Trail, from the left, joins the trail.

17.4 Begin a nasty, rocky, steep descent that lasts 0.2 mile.

17.9 The trail becomes a rough dirt road and goes slightly downhill.

18.3 Go through a swinging gate.

19.9 Turn right (south) onto US 550.

21.6 Turn right onto Hermosa Park Road, heading slightly uphill on gravel.

22.0 Reach an intersection with the ski area parking lot visible ahead.

22.1 Your car.

Cascade Divide to Relay Creek

[See map on page 91]

Location: A loop around Graysill Mountain, in the San Juan National Forest.

Distance: 28.5-mile loop.

Time: 3 to 5.5 hours.

Tread: 12.5 miles on gravel road; 7.8 miles on rough dirt road; 2.8 miles on singletrack; 5.4 miles on doubletrack or abandoned road.

Aerobic level: Strenuous, due to the length and a short climb on Colorado Trail.

Technical difficulty: Mostly 2, some 3 and 4.

Hazards: The route is a little difficult to find from Graysill Mine to Relay Creek Road. This route is totally above 10,000 feet, so be prepared for high altitude—no air and potential weather problems.

Highlights: This route is totally above 10,000 feet, and offers some great views—everything from Engineer Mountain to the Needles to Lizard Head to Hermosa Peak to the La Platas.

Land status: San Juan National Forest.

Maps: San Juan National Forest; USGS Engineer Mountain, Hermosa Peak.

Access: From Durango drive 25 miles north on U.S. Highway 550 to the Purgatory Resort turnoff. Go left (west) uphill on the paved road. In 0.4 mile turn away from the resort village and go north onto Hermosa Park Road (Forest Road 578). Go 3.5 miles and turn right (north) on Relay Creek Road (FR 580). Follow FR 580 1.3 miles to the intersection with Cascade Divide Road (FR 579), and park in the vicinity.

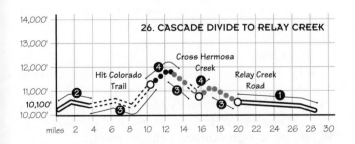

The ride:

0.0   Pedal north on Cascade Divide Road (FR 579), a smooth one-lane gravel road that soon bends east, climbing gradually.

1.8   The road descends with views of Grayrock Peak (to the northwest), Engineer Mountain (to the north), and the Twilight Peaks (to the east). For the next 6.8 miles, the road makes short descents and climbs as it contours around Graysill Mountain.

3.8   End downhill. The road from here gets rougher, but is still easily rideable.

7.1   Cross EZ Creek.

8.5   Cross Graysill Creek and go up a fairly steep hill.

8.8   Ignore a trail crossing the road here (see Ride 25). The road becomes steeper from this point.

9.1   Negotiate the first of two switchbacks as the climb continues.

10.7   Reach the end of the road and continue straight (northwest) on singletrack.

10.8   Watch carefully for a trail going left uphill at a 120-degree angle from the trail you're on. This is the Colorado Trail (CT), our next leg. If you miss this turn you will start going downhill and should turn around. The CT is mostly rideable, with a few tricky rocky or rooted sections.

11.8   Enjoy a very short downhill as the trail breaks above timberline.

12.5   The trail becomes rocky and steep, and difficult to ride.

12.6   Reach the top, surprisingly, and roll downhill (north).

13.0   Veer left onto doubletrack. Enjoy the view straight ahead of Lizard Head, and to its left, the Wilsons.

13.7   Come to a dirt road and turn left (south).

14.3 Watch for a trail going left. If you miss it, you'll still come out on Bolam Pass Road.

14.5 Turn left onto Bolam Pass Road at a small lake.

14.8 At a right-hand switchback just before the old Graysill Mine, turn left onto an unmarked old road. It climbs steeply for 100 yards, then levels out. For the next 2.2 miles, the road maintains approximately the same altitude, with short climbs and descents.

14.9 Cross Hermosa Creek and continue a short way on singletrack.

15.1 Join an abandoned road.

15.2 At a junction, veer right (south) and downhill on an abandoned road.

15.4 Go right and steeply downhill off the abandoned road on singletrack.

15.5 Pick up the abandoned road again and go uphill.

16.1 Another abandoned road joins in from the left. Twenty yards later, cross a small creek.

17.0 The road bends east and starts downhill.

18.5 Cross a small creek and head southwest on a rocky section of road.

19.8 Maneuver around a road-closure gate and come out on Relay Creek Road (FR 580). Turn left (southwest) and uphill on the smooth gravel road.

20.7 Top out on the climb. The road rises and falls as it goes in and out of drainages for the next 6.2 miles.

26.9 Top out on the last climb. Enjoy the last descent.

28.5 Reach the intersection of FR 579 and 580, and your car.

Molas to Coal Bank

Location: In the San Juan Mountains, from Molas Pass west on the Colorado Trail, west of Jura Knob, and over to Coal Bank Pass.

Distance: 17.4 miles point to point.

Time: 3 to 5 hours.

Tread: All singletrack.

Aerobic level: Strenuous.

Technical difficulty: Some 3, a lot of 4, and some 4+.

Hazards: Weather can change quickly—be prepared. You're a long way from help. The downhill just west of Jura Knob is steep and fairly technical, although mostly rideable.

Highlights: This is a beautiful high-altitude ride that gets rave reviews by almost everyone who rides it. Wildflowers peak during July and August.

Land status: San Juan National Forest.

Maps: San Juan National Forest; USGS Snowdon Peak, Silverton, Ophir, Engineer Mountain.

Access: To avoid cycling on U.S. Highway 550, do this ride as a shuttle. From Durango drive about 32 miles north on US 550 to the top of Coal Bank Pass and leave a vehicle here. In a second vehicle, continue north 8 miles to the Molas Pass parking area and overlook on the right. Park here and begin the ride by rolling north on US 550.

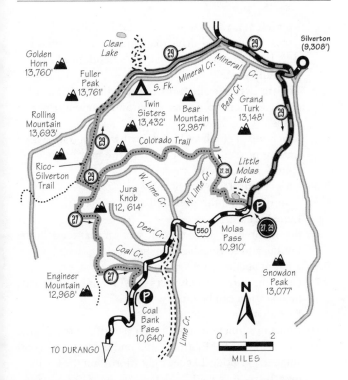

27. MOLAS TO COAL BANK
29. MOLAS TO SILVERTON

The ride:

0.0 Ride slowly down the north side of Molas Pass, watching for cars and the Colorado Trail (CT).

0.2 Look for the CT heading uphill, west off the highway. If you get to the gravel road heading to Little Molas Lake, you've gone too far.

0.9   Veer left at a Y junction next to Little Molas Lake.

1.1   Cross a four-wheel-drive road and to the CT on other side. Head slightly uphill on fairly smooth tread leading generally west.

2.4   The trail veers right (north) along the top of a ridge above timberline. Enjoy panoramic view of the San Juans.

3.2   Reach top of climb and head northwest on trail, which for the next 5.4 miles contours the mountainsides. Climbs and descents are short.

5.6   Cross North Lime Creek.

6.3   Spin through a fun downhill and cross a fork of West Lime Creek.

8.6   Begin climbing up a difficult section that tends to be muddy and unrideable in spots.

9.3   Top out at a large rock cairn.

9.7   Cross the narrow headwaters of West Lime Creek. This next section can be mucky.

10.1   Pass a tarn on the right.

10.6   Come to a junction and turn left (south) on the Engine Creek/Engineer Mountain Trail and continue up good singletrack. (Ride 29 goes right (north) on the CT from here.)

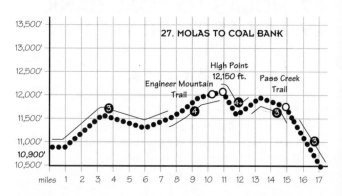

10.8 Hit the high point of the ride and roll gently downhill across alpine tundra. The trail should be easy to follow. Jura Knob is on the left.

11.1 The trail gets steeper and rougher as it descends toward Engine Creek. Enjoy views of Engineer Mountain to the south and Graysill Mountain to the southwest. The trail goes west briefly, then turns south and loops through a set of difficult switchbacks.

11.9 The trail levels out at the junction of Engineer Mountain and White Creek trails. Go left (east) on the Engineer Mountain track.

12.0 Begin to climb again. The next 0.7 mile is mostly rideable, but expect to dismount and push in a few spots.

12.7 The major climb ends, although there is one more small hill to come.

13.2 Roll onto a wide saddle with 12,968-foot Engineer Mountain looming large almost directly south.

14.0 Drop into a small meadow, the upper Coal Creek drainage, then begin a short climb.

14.8 At a junction at the base of Engineer Mountain, take the Pass Creek Trail left (east) down a fun singletrack section. This is a popular hiking trail, so yield to those on foot. (The Engineer Mountain Trail continues south, and offers an optional escape route. To go out this way, park a car near Cascade Creek and US 550. When the trail comes out on US 550, continue south and downhill on the highway to your car.)

16.2 Ride past a pond on the right.

17.1 Get glimpse of Coal Bank Pass through the trees.

17.4 Come to end of the trail and turn left onto the gravel road, which leads directly to Coal Bank Pass and your vehicle.

Bolam Pass to Hotel Draw

Location: Northwest of Purgatory in the San Juan Mountains.

Distance: 23.4 miles round trip.

Time: 3.5 to 5 hours.

Tread: 8.1 miles on slightly rough dirt road; 10 on miles singletrack; 1.5 miles on rocky dirt road; 3.8 miles on smooth, fast dirt road.

Aerobic level: Strenuous.

Technical difficulty: 3, with a few sections of 4 and 4+.

Hazards: Near Blackhawk Mountain you're a long way from help, and the weather can get nasty. Be prepared for the worst. The downhill off Blackhawk Mountain ridge is dicey in a couple of spots.

Highlights: A great high-altitude ride with spectacular views.

Land status: San Juan National Forest.

Maps: San Juan National Forest, USGS Hermosa Peak.

Access: From Durango drive 25 miles north on U.S. Highway 550 and turn left (west) toward Purgatory Resort. Go 0.4 mile and then turn away from the resort village and onto Forest Road 578. Continue 10.1 miles to a crossing of Hermosa Creek, which in early summer can be tricky. Keep some momentum. Park on the other side of the creek.

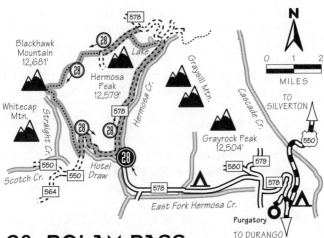

28. BOLAM PASS
TO HOTEL DRAW

The ride:

0.0   Pedal uphill and north on a dirt road, which is FR 578 or the Bolam Pass Road.

0.9   Veer right and downhill at a junction, staying on FR 578. The road on the left, FR 550, comes from Hotel Draw and is our return route.

4.7   Come to the first of many switchbacks. The climb gets a little steeper from here.

6.8   Pass the old Graysill Mine on the right. Enjoy a great view south of the La Plata Mountains. The route runs at an elevation of over 11,000 feet for the next 10 miles.

7.2   Go left (south) off the road just before a small lake, and look for the Colorado Trail going southwest. Climb on the singletrack trail.

8.8 Veer right onto doubletrack for 100 yards to a rocky, dirt road. Take the road left (southwest) and downhill.

9.5 Enjoy the view right (northwest) down into Barlow Creek.

10.3 Near the top of a rise turn right (west) off the road and onto singletrack, actually still the Colorado Trail. Climb.

11.3 Reach a high point (called Section Point on the map) and start downhill (northwest) along a ridge.

11.4 The trail turns off the ridge at an obvious spot. It heads south to contour around a hillside.

12.8 After some switchbacks, reach a low point—in elevation, hopefully not in energy.

13.5 Begin a steep, steady, rocky, technical climb. That said, a good rider can handle most of it.

14.4 Roll onto a saddle on the east side of Blackhawk Mountain. It's all downhill from here! Cross over to the Straight Creek drainage, heading steeply down rocky singletrack to the southeast. The first switchback is extremely difficult. Before you take off, enjoy the best views of the ride. Lizard Head is almost due north, with the Wilson range to its left.

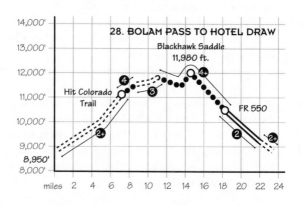

15.6 After a short stretch below timberline, the trail becomes much smoother.

18.7 Come to FR 550 and go left (north) and downhill in the Hotel Draw valley on the usually smooth dirt road.

22.5 Go right at the intersection with the Bolam Pass Road (FR 578; see mile 0.9 above).

23.4 Reach the car and those cold *cervezas* stashed in the ice box.

Molas to Silverton
[See map on page 99]

Location: San Juan Mountains, from Molas Pass west on the Colorado Trail, then down toward Silverton.

Distance: 29.9-mile loop.

Time: 4 to 6 hours.

Tread: 13.8 miles on singletrack; 0.7 mile on abandoned road; 2.6 miles on four-wheel-drive road; 4.4 miles on good gravel road; 8.4 miles on pavement.

Aerobic level: Strenuous.

Technical difficulty: A lot of 3, some 4 and 4+.

Hazards: Weather can change quickly—be prepared. You're a long way from help. The downhill section beginning at mile 11.3 is rocky, steep, and fairly technical.

Highlights: An excellent high-country ride, much above timberline with fantastic views.

Land status: San Juan National Forest.

Maps: San Juan National Forest; USGS Snowdon Peak, Silverton, Ophir.

Access: From Durango drive 40 miles north on U.S. Highway 550 to the top of Molas Pass. Park in the overlook parking area on the right (east).

The ride:

0.0 Ride slowly down the north side of Molas Pass, watching for cars and the Colorado Trail.

0.2 Look for the Colorado Trail heading uphill, west off the highway. If you get to the gravel road heading to Little Molas Lake, you've gone too far.

0.9 Veer left at a Y junction next to Little Molas Lake.

1.1 Cross a four-wheel-drive road and to the Colorado Trail on other side. Head slightly uphill on fairly smooth tread leading generally west.

2.4 The trail veers right (north) along the top of a ridge above timberline. Enjoy panoramic view of the San Juans.

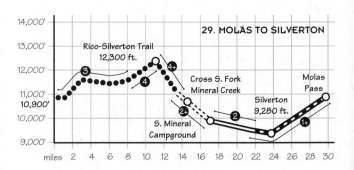

3.2 Reach top of climb and head northwest on trail, which for the next 5.4 miles contours the mountainsides. Climbs and descents are short.

5.6 Cross North Lime Creek.

6.3 Spin through a fun downhill and cross a fork of West Lime Creek.

8.6 Begin climbing up a difficult section that tends to be muddy and unrideable in spots.

9.3 Top out at a large rock cairn.

9.7 Cross the narrow headwaters of West Lime Creek. This next section can be mucky.

10.1 Pass a tarn on the right.

10.6 Come to a junction and turn right (north), continuing on the Colorado Trail. The trail continues to climb. (Ride 27 goes left (south) on the Engine Creek/Engineer Mountain Trail.)

11.3 Look to the right for rock cairns and posts marking the Rico-Silverton Trail down through the tundra. Take it, leaving the Colorado Trail. This next section is rocky and steep, and most riders will have to dismount in several places. (From the junction of the Colorado Trail and Rico-Silverton it's just a short ride on the Colorado Trail to a saddle with great views of Grizzly Peak and Cascade Creek.)

13.4 Finally, the trail flattens out at South Park.

13.8 Cross the South Fork of Mineral Creek and come to an old rocky road.

14.5 Cross the South Fork of Mineral Creek on a log and descend northeast on a fast, narrow dirt road (FR 585). It's tempting to really cruise in several stretches, but keep an eye out for oncoming traffic.

17.1 Come to South Mineral Campground (where water should be available). From here a wide gravel road leads to the highway.

21.5 Come to US 550 and go right (southeast) and downhill toward Silverton.
23.6 Stay on US 550 as it nears Silverton, then turns up Molas Pass. (An obvious option would be to park one car in Silverton before the ride. Or, send the lucky person who isn't exhausted up Molas to go get the car.)
29.9 Reach the top of Molas Pass and the parking lot.

Clear Lake

Location: West of Silverton, in the San Juan Mountains.

Distance: 5.3 miles one way.

Time: 1.5 to 3 hours.

Tread: 5.3 miles on four-wheel-drive road.

Aerobic level: Strenuous, with a constant steep climb.

Technical difficulty: Mostly 2; 3 near the top.

Hazards: It's easy to reach high speeds on the descent. Use caution and ride in control.

Highlights: A beautiful high mountain lake. Although steep, the road is fairly smooth and not horribly long.

Land status: San Juan National Forest.

Maps: San Juan National Forest, USGS Ophir.

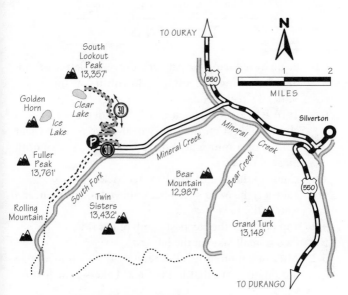

30. CLEAR LAKE

Access: From Durango drive 50 miles north on U.S. Highway 550 to Silverton. At a Y intersection on the outskirts of town veer left, staying on US 550. From that point drive 2 miles and take a left on South Mineral Creek Road (County Road 7). Go another 4.2 miles to the Ice Lakes Trailhead parking lot, which is on the north side of the road opposite South Mineral Creek Campground. (The Clear Lake turnoff is 0.6 mile before the parking lot, but it's best to use the Ice Lakes parking lot. There's an outhouse and water here, and a better place for your vehicle.)

The ride:

0.0 Begin by retracing the path you drove. Go left (east) out of the parking lot, slightly downhill, on the South Mineral Creek Road.

0.6 Turn left, turning back nearly 180 degrees to begin climbing west on the four-wheel-drive road to Clear Lake. For a four-wheel-drive track, it's very smooth most of the way.

1.6 Come to the first of many switchbacks.

4.1 Take a right-hand switchback above timberline near a waterfall.

4.9 Top out after the steepest climb of the ride.

5.0 Pass a small lake on the left.

5.3 After one more brief climb the road rolls into a huge mountain basin that holds Clear Lake—your just reward.

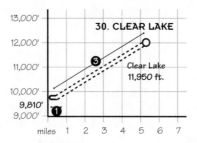

Placer to Picayne

Location: Northeast of Silverton in the San Juan Mountains.

Distance: 9.4-mile loop.

Time: 1.5 to 3 hours.

Tread: 9.4 miles on four-wheel-drive road.

Aerobic level: Strenuous.

Technical difficulty: 3+.

Hazards: High altitude, a steep descent.

Highlights: Most of the ride is above timberline, offering great views. You'll see a couple mining ghost towns and get a great workout. The downhill is a blast if there's not much four-wheel-drive traffic.

Land status: Bureau of Land Management, private (old mining claims).

Maps: San Juan National Forest, USGS Handies Peak.

Access: From Durango drive 50 miles north on U.S. Highway 550 to Silverton and veer right onto Colorado Highway 110, which becomes Forest Road 586. Go 1 mile, taking a right onto CO 110 just past downtown Silverton. Go 10.8 miles up CO 110, which becomes gravel and then dwindles to a one-lane rough dirt road. There are good parking spots on the left just after the Picayne Gulch turnoff.

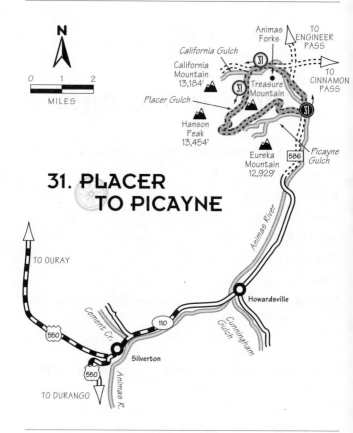

31. PLACER TO PICAYNE

The ride:

0.0 Head uphill and north on FR 586, the Cinnamon Pass Road.

0.7 Ignore a steep uphill road right. Instead, veer left and continue toward Animas Forks.

1.5 At the ghost town of Animas Forks, go left (northwest) up California Gulch Road.

2.6 Turn left (south) onto Placer Gulch Road, and immediately cross California Gulch, usually low and rideable.

3.9 The road becomes steeper and rockier. This is where most riders start to feel the elevation.

4.5 Cross Placer Gulch at the old Gold Prince Mine. Don't let those steep switchbacks up ahead (south) deter you. They're a challenge, but if you're in good shape, they're all rideable.

5.3 The road flattens out momentarily as it turns east. The climbs aren't quite over, but the hard part is. From here the road contours along a high ridge, heading over toward Picayne Gulch.

5.7 At a break in the ridge to the right, stop and enjoy the view south. To the north, if you know where you're looking, the 14,000-foot Wetterhorn and Uncompahgre peaks are visible.

6.4 The downhill into Picayne Gulch begins in earnest as the road passes a knob (Treasure Mountain) on the left.

8.3 The grade becomes steeper, and your grip on the brakes

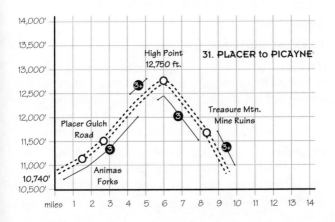

tighter, as the road passes the impressive Treasure Mountain Mine ruins on the right.

9.4 Welcome back to the starting point. Where's that tire iron so I can pry my hands off the brakes?

Haflin Creek

Location: Northeast of Durango, crossing from the east to the west side of Missionary Ridge, in the San Juan National Forest.

Distance: 23.8-mile loop.

Time: 3 to 4.5 hours.

Tread: 5.1 miles on singletrack; 3.2 miles on gravel road; 2.7 miles on dirt road; 12.8 miles on paved road.

Aerobic level: Strenuous.

Technical difficulty: Singletrack gets a 5.

Hazards: The 4.6 miles on Haflin Creek Trail are very technical—an endo waiting to happen. The trail is sometimes very narrow and in the last 2 miles often cambers toward a great abyss. There are several steep, rooted sections, several rock steps and several tight switchbacks. Use caution.

Highlights: Great technical downhill. If you can clean it, you're a stud or studette. This ride makes most others seem easy. Good views of the Animas River valley. Good training climb. This is a Durango-area highlight.

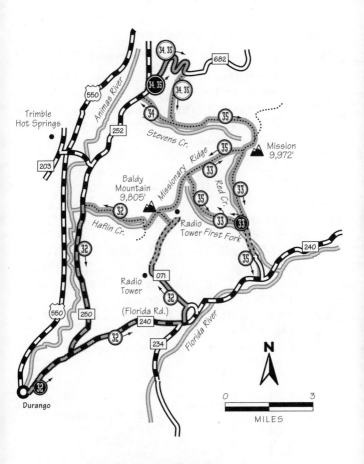

32. HAFLIN CREEK
33. FIRST FORK
34. STEVENS CREEK
35. STEVENS TO FIRST FORK

Land status: San Juan National Forest.

Maps: San Juan National Forest; USGS Durango East.

Access: From the corner of 15th Street and 3rd Avenue in Durango, take Florida Road northeast 0.5 mile to the Chapman Hill Ski Area parking lot on the right side of the road. You can start the ride from any place in town, but this is a good spot if you want to drive to a starting place.

The ride:

0.0 Pedal northeast on the paved Florida Road (County Road 240).

5.9 Turn left (north) onto CR 249 (Forest Road 071). This turn is 0.1 mile after passing the turn to CR 234 and comes after a fast downhill section. Begin a steep uphill on CR 249 on well-packed gravel.

6.2 Turn left (north) onto CR 249B (FR 071). If in doubt for the next 2.9 miles, stay on FR 071.

7.0 At an intersection, continue straight uphill.

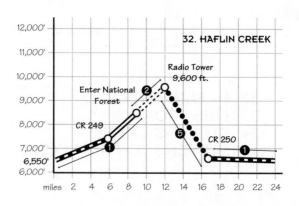

8.0 The steep climb ends (momentarily). Go downhill and west on FR 071.

8.2 Turn right, still on FR 071, and shift back into granny gear.

9.1 Go through a fence (which blocks motorized traffic) and enter the San Juan National Forest. There's a small parking area here (a hint for those who would rather do a shuttle and avoid some climbing). Continue uphill on a rough dirt road.

10.8 Enjoy clicking into your middle ring for a little downhill!

11.4 Come to a Y intersection under some power lines and veer left (north) onto a dirt road. In about 100 yards the Missionary Ridge Trail splits off to the right, but we stay on the dirt road.

11.8 Just before a radio tower, veer left (west) onto singletrack (the Missionary Ridge Trail) going downhill.

12.3 Turn right (north) off Missionary Ridge Trail and onto Haflin Creek Trail. Check your brakes. This is a difficult, technical downhill, with steep switchbacks, roots, rocks, and dropoffs, so use caution. The pros can ride the whole thing. Some of us with lesser skills choose not to.

13.8 Gradually the trail levels out a bit. This is a chance to make sure blood is still circulating in your hands.

15.1 Pass through a stock fence. The dirt here is red and the trail leaves Haflin Creek, which drops over a waterfall on the left.

15.6 Negotiate the first of three series of rock steps. From here the trail is narrow and exposed, leaning toward the abyss. And it gets steeper again.

16.9 Come to the Haflin Creek Trail parking lot and CR 250 (East Animas Road). Turn left and pedal south on the pavement.

22.3 Come to the end of CR 250 and a T intersection. Turn right onto Florida Road.

23.8 Return to Chapman Hill parking area.

First Fork

[See map on page 115]

Location: Northeast of Durango on the east side of Missionary Ridge, in the San Juan National Forest.

Distance: 10.9-mile loop (7.4-mile out-and-back, skipping the Red Creek Trail).

Time: 2 to 4 hours.

Tread: All singletrack except for 0.4 mile of dirt road on the loop.

Aerobic level: Strenuous.

Technical difficulty: 4 and 5.

Hazards: Logs across the trail, cow pies, technical downhills—especially on the loop—and possible creek crossings in the spring. This is a popular ride for horseback riders.

Highlights: Excellent backcountry adventure ride.

Land status: San Juan National Forest. Road access through private land.

Maps: San Juan National Forest; USGS Rules Hill, Durango East, Hermosa, and Lemon Reservoir.

Access: From the junction of East 3rd Avenue and 15th Street in Durango, drive 9.5 miles northeast on Florida Road (County Road 240) to a gravel road (CR 246) that breaks left (north) to Colvig Silver Camp. Follow this road, which turns from gravel to dirt, for 1.9 miles. Be on the lookout for the First Fork Trailhead on the left (west). You can park at the trailhead, but better spots are 0.1 mile back the way you came.

The ride:

0.0   Ford Red Creek and head west on First Fork Trail. In about 30 yards go through a stock fence.

0.7   Begin a series of short, technical climbs, some of which are unrideable. Hang in there, because it eventually does get easier.

1.8   Enter a nice aspen grove. Most sections here are rideable, and the tread is fairly smooth unless cattle have been through.

2.9   Enter an open meadow and begin a steep ascent. To the southwest is a radio tower on top of Missionary Ridge.

3.5   Take the switchback that goes 120 degrees uphill left (west). The trail going straight heads into Cabin Fork and disappears.

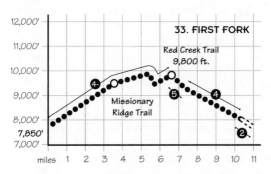

3.7 Reach Missionary Ridge Trail. For the out-and-back, turn around here. Those who want more, and are ready for a technical challenge, turn right (northeast) onto Missionary Ridge Trail and begin a steady uphill climb.

5.5 Begin a short downhill on the west side of the ridge.

5.9 Cross over to the east side of the ridge and continue down a steep, short section. In 0.1 mile the trail begins climbing again.

6.8 Turn right (south) onto Red Creek Trail. Begin a steep descent with tight switchbacks and loose rocks and dirt. Most folks walk their bikes down. Also at this intersection, ignore the rough trail going south-southwest.

7.3 The trail finally becomes more rideable, although there are more rocky sections where it's much safer to walk or carry your bike.

7.7 A welcome flat spot. The trail is still nasty in spots, but mellows out the lower it goes.

10.2 Pass an old metal wreckage (a drag line) on the left.

10.5 The trail becomes a dirt road. In 50 yards it hooks up with another dirt road coming from the left (north). This is the road you parked on.

10.9 Return to the First Fork Trailhead.

Stevens Creek

[See map on page 115]

Location: North of Durango on the west side of Missionary Ridge, in the San Juan National Forest.

Distance: 7.3-mile loop.

Time: 1 to 2 hours.

Tread: 3.7 miles on gravel road; 3.1 miles on singletrack; 0.5 mile on paved county road.

Aerobic level: Moderate.

Technical difficulty: Mostly 3, with some 4 and 4+.

Hazards: Missionary Ridge Road can be busy on weekends. Be very careful of traffic. There are a couple of technical sections on the singletrack downhill where most people walk their bikes. Also, hikers frequent the trail; ride in control and yield to other trail users.

Highlights: Good views down onto the Animas Valley and into the La Plata Mountains. The downhill singletrack is fun where it isn't nasty.

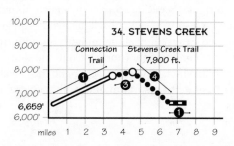

Land status: San Juan National Forest.

Maps: San Juan National Forest; USGS Hermosa.

Access: From Durango drive 8 miles north on U.S. Highway 550. Just after a right-hand bend in the road, turn right onto Trimble Lane (County Road 252). In 1 mile, turn left at a T intersection, still on CR 252, heading north. Go 3.1 miles and veer right onto gravel Missionary Ridge Road (Forest Road 682), heading slightly uphill. Park near the intersection on the shoulder of the road.

The ride:

0.0   Head north, slightly uphill on the well-graded Missionary Ridge Road.

1.5   Come to the first of several switchbacks. The road begins to steepen.

3.7   As the road enters a left-hand switchback, notice a dirt road going right (south) off the main road. Follow it 20 yards to where it dead-ends. Look for singletrack, which leads to Stevens Creek Trail. This connecting trail goes briefly downhill, contouring in and out of a drainage, then heads uphill.

4.3   Reach Stevens Creek Trail and decision time: Do we go right, downhill, making this a nice, easy ride? Or left, uphill for a granny-gear climb? Let's take the easy way and go right. (See Ride 35 to continue climbing.)

5.4   Watch for a sudden switchback just when you grew accustomed to speeding along on fairly smooth tread.

5.7   Pass a path on the right (north). Continue south on the main trail, which now gets steeper and more technical. Don't hesitate to dismount and walk a couple of sections.

6.8 Hit CR 252 and go right (north), on pavement.
7.3 Come to the Missionary Ridge Road turnoff, and your
car.

Stevens to First Fork
[See map on page 115]

Location: Northeast of Durango, crossing Missionary Ridge, in
the San Juan National Forest.

Distance: 19.9 miles point to point.

Time: 3.5 to 5 hours.

Tread: 4.7 miles on gravel road; 10 miles on singletrack; 4.2
miles on doubletrack; 1 mile on rough dirt road.

Aerobic level: Strenuous, due to a long climb.

Technical difficulty: Mostly 3, with some 4 and 5.

Hazards: These trails may not be well marked. The weather up
on the ridge can quickly get nasty.

Highlights: There are some very fun singletrack downhill sections. These trails don't get a lot of use, although you may see
horses and cattle around.

Land status: San Juan National Forest.

Maps: San Juan National Forest; USGS Hermosa, Lemon
Reservoir, Durango East, Rules Hill.

Access: This ride requires a shuttle, which is admittedly kind
of a drag. You can do it without a shuttle, but that means about

21 extra miles on pavement. An option would be to have two groups meet in the middle of the ride and exchange keys.

From the corner of 15th Street and 3rd Avenue in Durango, drive northeast 9.3 miles on Florida Road (County Road 240) to the Colvig Silver Camp turn. Go left onto CR 246 and park one car just off Florida Road.

Return to 32nd Street and Main Avenue in Durango and take U.S. Highway 550 north 8 miles. Just after a right-hand bend in the road, turn right onto Trimble Lane (CR 252). In 1 mile, turn left at a T intersection, still on CR 252, heading north. Go 3.1 miles and veer right onto Missionary Ridge Road (Forest Road 682), a gravel road heading slightly uphill. Park on the shoulder of the road near the intersection.

The ride:

0.0   Pedal north and slightly uphill on the well-graded Missionary Ridge Road.

1.5   Come to the first of several switchbacks. The road begins to steepen.

3.7   As the road enters a left-hand switchback, watch for a dirt road going right (south) off the main road. Follow

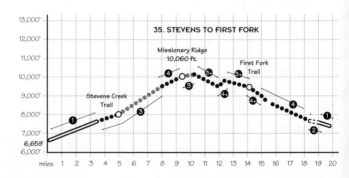

35. STEVENS TO FIRST FORK

Missionary Ridge
10,060 ft.

First Fork
Trail

Stevens Creek
Trail

it 20 yards to singletrack, which leads to Stevens Creek Trail. This connecting trail goes briefly downhill, contouring in and out of a drainage, then heads uphill.

4.3 Reach Stevens Creek Trail and go left (south) on a steady uphill grade.

5.0 An old road from the left meets the Stevens Creek Trail. Continue uphill on doubletrack.

6.2 The trail bends north to climb to a saddle.

6.4 At the saddle, go right (east). Going straight (northeast) leads to Wallace Lakes and back to Missionary Ridge Road.

7.3 The climb tapers momentarily, but 0.2 mile farther steepens again.

8.2 Reach singletrack, and the steepest part of the climb to Missionary Ridge.

9.2 At the top of a rise clotted with lots of down timber, look for a trail on the right (east). Follow it up another short climb to an old road and go right, slightly uphill.

9.5 Come to Missionary Ridge Trail and go right (south), on an old road grade. (If the weather is bad, or you're tired and not ready for an adventure, turn back here.)

10.2 Veer right off the old road grade and onto singletrack for some downhill fun.

11.1 Ignore the Red Creek Trail taking off left downhill (south). Veer right (northwest), staying on Missionary Ridge Trail and heading slightly downhill.

11.9 End a fun descent and begin a steep ascent, bike-pushing for 0.2 mile.

12.5 The climb ends.

14.2 After another fun downhill—watch for water bars—turn left (east) and downhill on First Fork Trail. Be wary, because the trail is easy to miss. Missionary Ridge Trail continues south, ascending again from here.

14.4 Watch for a 120-degree switchback turn right (south).

The trail going straight dead-ends. The singletrack gets tricky through here—rocky, steep, and technical in places.

15.0 As the trail bottoms out from a straight descent through a meadow the tread becomes less technical.

17.9 Go through a stock fence, cross Red Creek, and go right (south) downhill on a rough dirt road.

18.9 The road (now CR 246) becomes gravel and heads south, downhill.

19.9 The intersection of CR 246 and Florida Road, where you parked the shuttle car. Who has the keys?

Moonlick Park

Location: Northeast of Bayfield in the San Juan National Forest.

Distance: 19.1-mile loop.

Time: 2.5 to 3.5 hours.

Tread: 4.2 miles on gravel road; 14.9 miles on four-wheel-drive road.

Aerobic level: Moderate.

Technical difficulty: 2, with some 3 and 4.

Hazards: There are some large rocks and ruts in the downhill stretch on Moonlick Park Road. This is a popular big-game hunting area best avoided from mid-October to mid-November.

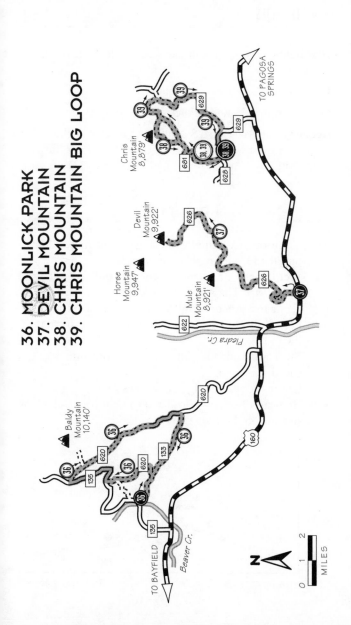

36. MOONLICK PARK
37. DEVIL MOUNTAIN
38. CHRIS MOUNTAIN
39. CHRIS MOUNTAIN BIG LOOP

Highlights: A good early or late-season ride thanks to its low elevation.

Land status: San Juan National Forest.

Maps: San Juan National Forest; USGS Baldy Mountain.

Access: From Bayfield go 8.2 miles east on U.S. Highway 160 to gravel Beaver Meadows Road (Forest Road 135). Turn left (north) and go 2.7 miles to Ute Park Road (FR 133) and park.

The ride:

0.0 Go through a swinging metal gate, heading southeast on FR 133, a four-wheel-drive road.

0.2 Veer left and uphill at a Y junction and veer left again at mile 0.4. The road gets rockier and steeper.

1.7 Come to a junction and go left (east) on FR 160, heading uphill. Your return will be via the right-hand road, FR 133.

4.0 FR 160-B1 heads left; instead, continue straight (north).

4.2 Ignore the road going 120 degrees right.

4.9 Hit Beaver Meadows Road and go right (east), climbing steadily on the wide gravel road.

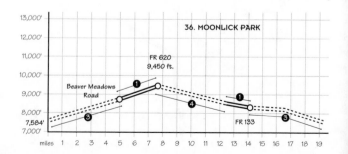

5.6 The road turns north.

7.6 Turn right onto Moonlick Park Road (FR 620), and pedal east up a slight grade.

7.7 The four-wheel-drive road gets rockier, veers right (south), and heads downhill.

11.1 A road joins FR 620 from the left. Continue south, veering right.

11.2 Go through a wire stock fence and enter an extremely rocky section.

12.5 FR 620 becomes First Notch Road, a wide, maintained gravel road on which you can get going frighteningly fast.

14.0 As the road leans into a right-hand turn, the turnoff for FR 133 is on the right (west). Take this good dirt road downhill.

15.0 At a junction, stay left, taking the less-defined road.

16.4 Go through a swinging metal gate.

17.4 Hit a junction (same as mile 1.7) and go left (west) on FR 160.

19.1 Go through the metal gate and find your awaiting auto.

Devil Mountain

[See map on page 127]

Location: Between Bayfield and Pagosa Springs, east above the Piedra River drainage, in the San Juan National Forest.

Distance: 24.4-mile out-and-back (12.2 miles one way.)

Time: 3 to 5 hours total.

Tread: 24.4 miles on one-lane dirt road.

Aerobic level: Strenuous.

Technical difficulty: 2. The road is mostly smooth with a couple of rocky sections.

Hazards: It's easy to get going *very* fast on the return, so be wary of the rare auto.

Highlights: That *very* fast downhill. Although the road gains almost 3,300 feet, there are no extreme climbs. From the top, views are good looking north and west.

Land status: San Juan National Forest, with a short section passing through private land.

Maps: San Juan National Forest; USGS Chimney Rock, Devil Mountain.

Access: From Bayfield drive 21 miles east on U.S. Highway 160 to Devil Mountain Road (Forest Road 626). Turn left here and find a good parking spot. To reduce the amount of climbing, drive a ways up the road, which is usually in good shape for all vehicles nearly the entire way.

The ride:

0.0   Begin climbing north on Devil Mountain Road, a dirt road that is generally smooth.
4.5   Veer right (east) at a junction.
5.1   The road narrows and gets a little rougher as it swings left (northwest) and begins a short downhill.
5.8   The downhill ends as the road bends east.
9.8   The road swings around to a north-northwest heading.
11.9 Ride over granite and come to a Y junction. Right (north-northeast) leads to the top of Devil Mountain. Left (northwest) goes to a much better lookout point. For this guide, go left. Either way is short enough to easily do both.
12.2 Come to a weather tower and enjoy views north toward the Weminuche Wilderness off in the distance and west toward the Piedra River. This road keeps going but deteriorates. Best to turn back here.
24.4 Retrace your tracks to return to the junction of Devil Mountain Road and US 160.

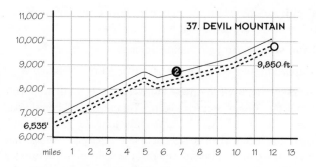

Chris Mountain

[See map on page 127]

Location: About 10 miles west of Pagosa Springs, on the San Juan National Forest.

Distance: 11.2-mile out-and-back with a loop on top of Chris Mountain.

Time: 1.5 to 2.5 hours.

Tread: 7 miles on fairly smooth dirt road, 4.2 miles on rough dirt road.

Aerobic level: Moderate.

Technical difficulty: 2, with a couple of short sections of 3.

Hazards: The downhill on the loop may be a little rocky, and some large humps across the tread make good launching pads. Watch for motorcycles and ATVs.

Highlights: A relatively mellow ride in a nice forest. Views from the top are somewhat limited by trees.

Land status: San Juan National Forest.

Maps: San Juan National Forest; USGS Chris Mountain.

Access: From Bayfield drive 33 miles east on U.S. Highway 160. Turn left at Turkey Springs Trading Post onto gravel Forest Road 629 (Badger Road). Veer left at 0.3 mile from the pavement and again at mile 0.6. Then go right at mile 1.1 (left goes onto private land). At 1.6 miles, just after entering the national forest, turn left onto FR 628 (Snow Ranch Road). Follow this road 2 miles to FR 681 (Chris Mountain Road) on the right. Go up FR 681 about 10 yards; there is a good parking place on the right.

The ride:

0.0   Begin climbing west on Chris Mountain Road, a fairly smooth dirt road. The climb is fairly steady, with a couple of short breaks.

3.5   Come to a junction on the edge of a large meadow. This is the start of the loop, and either direction is about the same. For this guide, continue straight (east). Either way, from here the tread becomes doubletrack and rougher.

5.0   A road takes off to the right (east); instead, continue on the main road that goes north and begins to bend toward the west. The road levels out from here, climbing only a few more feet. (See Ride 39, mile 5.0, if you'd like to take the road going east.)

5.7   The doubletrack begins its descent down Chris Mountain.

7.7   Return to the large meadow and junction. Go right (west) downhill, back from whence you came.

11.2 Back at your car.

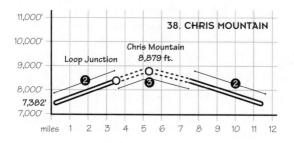

Chris Mountain
Big Loop
[See map on page 127]

Location: About 10 miles west of Pagosa Springs, on the San Juan National Forest.

Distance: 12.4-mile loop.

Time: 1.5 to 3 hours.

Tread: 7.1 miles on easy dirt road; 3.3 miles on sometimes rocky doubletrack; 2 miles on gravel road.

Aerobic level: Moderate.

Technical difficulty: 2, with some 3+ on the descent off Chris Mountain.

Hazards: Coming down Forest Road 629 is one of the fastest dirt descents I've ever seen. Be very careful—it may seem you have the road to yourself, but the occasional vehicle makes for a nasty surprise.

Highlights: This is a pretty good, out-of-the-way ride. Nothing spectacular, but solidly fun.

Land status: San Juan National Forest.

Maps: San Juan National Forest; USGS Chris Mountain, Lonetree Canyon.

Access: From Bayfield drive 33 miles east on U.S. Highway 160. Turn left at Turkey Springs Trading Post onto gravel FR

629 (Badger Road). Veer left at 0.3 mile and 0.6 mile in from the pavement. Then go right at mile 1.1 (left goes onto private land). At 1.6 miles, just after entering the national forest, turn left onto FR 628 (Snow Ranch Road). Follow this road 2 miles to FR 681 (Chris Mountain Road) on the right. Go up FR 681 about 10 yards; there is a good parking place on the right.

The ride:

0.0 Begin climbing west on Chris Mountain Road. The climb is fairly steady, with a couple of short breaks.

3.5 Come to a junction on the edge of a large meadow. For a little longer ride, turn left (northwest) and go 2.7 miles, then jump to mile 5.0 below. To follow this guide, continue straight (east). From here the tread becomes doubletrack and rougher.

5.0 Just as you top a climb, on a fairly flat section, turn right on a road that goes east off the main road. Take this old road as it winds down the east side of Chris Mountain, gently at first, then steeply as it becomes rockier.

6.7 Pass through a stock fence.

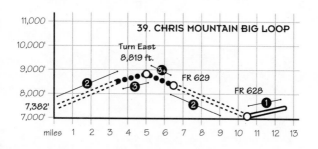

6.8 Come to FR 629 at what appears to be a three-way junction. Go right (southwest) and downhill on FR 629. The next 3.6 miles is very fast and can be fun, but remember there are cars around.

9.5 Ignore a private road going right (northwest) off the main road. This is right in the middle of a screaming descent, so if you read this beforehand, you can rest pretty much assured that you won't miss the next turn.

10.4 At a three-way junction, turn right (north) off FR 629 and onto FR 628 (Snow Ranch Road). You drove in this way, remember? Begin a steady climb back to the junction with Chris Mountain Road.

12.4 Return to the starting point.

Appendix A:

Other Durango-area Routes

Yes, there's more. Some of the best stuff hasn't been mentioned, because it can't really be mapped. Durango Mountain Park listed below, for instance, has myriad trails, but you've got to go explore. Telling you exactly where to go would be rude, wouldn't it?

You may have noticed a dearth of easy rides in the 39 rides previously discussed. Some possible beginning-type rides are given below.

The second group of trails are mentioned here solely to warn mountain bikers to stay away from them. These routes may be too rocky, steep, erodible, or chronically muddy. If you want to travel these trails, go on foot (call it cross training).

Alternate Routes

Telegraph Trail

Location: Same start as for Ride 1, The Ridge. Just east of town, Telegraph Trail goes up and over a low ridge, with ponderosa pine, juniper, and scrub oak the main vegetation.
Distance: 9.8-mile loop.
Time: 50 minutes to 1.5 hours.
Tread: 0.9 mile on rough dirt road; 4.0 miles on singletrack; 2.7 miles on abandoned road that could be considered singletrack; 2.2 miles on paved highway.
Aerobic level: Moderate, although the Telegraph Trail climb is long.
Technical difficulty: Mostly 3, some 4-.
Hazards: Watch for traffic as this trail is becoming the most popular in town. People ride it both ways, so beware of places with limited vision. Horseback riders use a section of Sidewinder Trail. Tall people definitely want to duck under an overhanging rock on Telegraph Trail.

Highlights: Easy access, good workout, nice views of town and La Plata Mountains.
Land status: County road, La Plata County easement through private property, Bureau of Land Management, state highway. As this book went to press, the county was still in the process of acquiring easements from the land-owner for many sections of this trail, constructed in 1996 and 1997. If all went well, this ride should all be on public land. In any case, please obey all no trespassing signs — the landowner has been very generous to allow this trail across the property.
Maps: USGS Durango East, Loma Linda.
Access: Southeast of downtown Durango, find the intersection of 8th Avenue and 3rd Street. Go east on 3rd Street, which turns into Horse Gulch Road in a block. There is limited parking.

The ride:

0.0 Head east up Horse Gulch Road, climbing fairly steeply. Pass a spur on the left.
0.7 Turn right (southeast) off Horse Gulch, going a short distance downhill on a dirt road. Continue on this road after it crosses a small ditch. (For Ride 1, continue up Horse Gulch Road. See page 19)
0.9 Take a left (east) onto the singletrack Telegraph Trail, which heads downhill momentarily, then begins a slight climb through a large meadow.
1.4 An indistinct trail here goes left (north). Continue straight (east) toward the ridge ahead, beginning a steeper climb.
1.9 Cross a ravine and begin heading southwest, contouring up the ridge.
2.3 After a switchback, watch for a rock overhanging the trail. Continue to climb.
2.8 Top out after a short, very steep climb that makes most riders go anaerobic. For this loop, continue straight (east). For a quick way back to Horse Gulch, go 20 yards from the top-out and take a left onto the Anasazi Descent.
3.0 After a short downhill, the Crites Connection will be on your right as you begin another uphill. Continue

straight. (The Crites Connection is a 1.6-mile track — 0.5 mile on an old road, 1.1 miles of new singletrack — that will take you to mile 5.5 below. The Crites is a fun, twisting descent —watch for low, overhanging branches and steep sidehills.)

3.2 Start down what's known as the "suicide" section, so-called because to ride up it used to be considered deadly.

3.5 At the bottom of the "suicide" section, turn right (south) onto an old road which these days passes for singletrack. From here to the Carbon Junction Trail the route has been dubbed the Sidewinder Trail. The Sidewinder is a slightly downhill, extremely fun section with fast turns. Do use caution, considering there could be other traffic.

5.5 Come to an intersection, with the Carbon Junction Trail on the left (south) and Crites Connection to your right (north). Go left on Carbon Junction Trail, a fun, rocky, singletrack descent that skirts to the east of an operat ing gravel pit.

7.6 Descend onto Colorado Highway 3 and go right (north). This eventually becomes 8th Avenue.

9.8 Take a right onto 3rd Street, assuming you parked at the start.

Durango Mountain Park—This area, west of town and an-nexed by the city, is informally known as the "Test Track." There are several access points, but the easiest way to get there is to go west on 22nd St. from Main Avenue in Durango and don't turn off, even when it goes up a steep, paved hill and becomes Montview Parkway. Among other access points in the area are Leyden Street and Crestview Av-enue.

There are several singletrack trails in the park. Many have short, steep climbs which test your fitness. Others have turns and obstacles which test your ability or your bike.

La Plata Canyon—There are several steep jeep roads leading up from La Plata Canyon Road. If you're out to get in shape for high-altitude riding, this is one way to do it. A couple of routes here are featured rides in this book — Eagle Pass (Ride 10) and The Notch (Ride 11) — but there are many more possibilities.

1990 Worlds Course—This starts at the base of Purgatory Resort, and is basically the course of the first UCI-sanctioned World Championships of mountain biking, held in 1990. The resort puts signs on the mountain in the summer to guide riders along the course; it's not exactly the same course, but it's close, and it certainly lets you understand the challenges — steep climbs at high altitude and a couple of steep, tricky descents.

Iron Horse Course—This incorporates portions of The Ridge (Ride 1) and the Chapman Hill Loop (Ride 2), and cuts across the Fort Lewis College campus. It's a great race course, but uses chunks of private land, where mountain bikes are sometimes not allowed. For up-to-date information, local bike shops should know the land status.

Road Apple—When it's cold in Durango, try visiting this playground of smooth rolling hills in Farmington, New Mexico. Go south on U.S. Highway 550 about 50 miles to the outskirts of Farmington. Take a right onto Piñon Hills Boulevard and head for the Lion's Amphitheater just north of San Juan Community College. Park there and ride, generally north. There's a lot of land out there, so don't get lost.

Moab—It's not that far away! See Mountain Biking Moab for descriptions of all the classic canyon, slick rock, and La Sal rides.

Easier Rides

Horse Gulch—Follow the directions for Ride 1, but go up only as far as you feel comfortable on Horse Gulch Road. Then turn around and come back.

Dry Fork Road—Follow the directions for Ride 6, but park at the intersection of Lightner Creek Road and Dry Fork Road, and ride as far as you feel like from there.

Hermosa Creek out-and-back—Follow directions for Ride 18 for parking a shuttle car at the south end of Hermosa Creek Trail. Park at the south end and go up the trail a ways, then return. The first several miles are fairly mellow.

Trails NOT Recommended
for Mountain Bike Use

Perin's Peak—West of Durango. As tempting as it is, this ride is on Colorado Division of Wildlife land and off-limits to mountain bikers. You'll get a stiff fine if caught on land east of County Road 208 (Dry Fork Road).

Shearer Creek—This one almost went in the book, but it's so rough and muddy and rocky that it's really too difficult to enjoy. Shearer Creek is in the Missionary Ridge vicinity, and is a little tricky to find from the top. It's easy to get lost when coming from the bottom, also. My advice: leave this to the horses.

Weminuche Wilderness—There are several ways to enter the Weminuche Wilderness on trails. Please do not be tempted. Bicycles are illegal in designated wilderness areas, and there are plenty of other rides. (At least 39 of them!)

Appendix B

Information Sources

San Juan National Forest
Visitor Information
701 Camino del Rio
Durango CO 81301
(970) 247-4874

Columbine Ranger District
110 W. 11th St.
Durango, CO 81301
(970) 247-4874

Pine Ranger District
367 S. Pearl St.
Bayfield, CO 81122
(970) 884-2512

Bureau of Land Management
701 Camino del Rio
Durango, CO 81301
(970) 247-4082

Colorado Division of Wildlife
151 E. 16th St.
Durango, CO 81301
(970) 247-0855

Trails 2000
(local trails advocacy group)
P.O. Box 3868
Durango, CO 81302
(970) 259-4682

Durango Area Chamber Resort Association
111 S. Camino del Rio
P.O. Box 2587
Durango, CO 81301
(970) 247-0312
1-800-463-8726

Bayfield Area Chamber of Commerce
381-5 E. Colorado Drive
Bayfield, CO 81122
(970) 884-9782

Silverton Chamber of Commerce
418 Greene St.
P.O. Box 565
Silverton, CO 81433
(970) 387-5654

Centura Health-Mercy Medical Center
375 E. Park Ave.
Durango, CO 81301
(970) 247-4311

IMBA
P.O. Box 7578
Boulder, CO 80306-7578
(303) 545-9011
IMBAjim@aol.com

Bike Shops

Mountain Bike Specialists
949 Main Ave.
Durango, CO 81301
(970) 247-4066

Durango Cyclery
143 E. 13th St.
Durango, CO 81301
(970) 247-0747

Hard Line Sports
1139 Main Ave.
Durango, CO 81301
(970) 259-9141

Hassle Free Sports
2615 Main Ave.
Durango, CO 81301
(970) 259-3874

Pedal the Peaks
598B Main Ave.
Durango, CO 81301
(970) 259-6880
(800) 743-3843

Glossary

ATB: All-terrain bicycle; a.k.a. mountain bike, sprocket rocket, fat tire flyer.

ATV: All-terrain vehicle; in this book ATV refers to motorbikes and three- and four-wheelers designed for off-road use.

Bail: Getting off the bike, usually in a hurry, and whether or not you meant to. Often a last resort.

Bonk: Running out of energy. Either you end up moving slowly, like in quicksand, or not at all—lying on the trail gasping for air.

Buffed: When tread is smooth and fast.

Bunny hop: Leaping up, while riding, and lifting both wheels off the ground to jump over an obstacle (or for sheer joy).

Clean: To ride without touching a foot (or other body part) to the ground; to ride a tough section successfully.

Contour: A line on a topographic map showing a continuous elevation level. Also used as a verb to indicate a fairly easy or moderate grade: "The trail contours around the west flank of the mountain before the final grunt to the top."

Dab: To put a foot or hand down (or hold onto or lean on a tree or other support) while riding. If you have to dab, then you haven't ridden that piece of trail **clean.**

Downfall: Trees that have fallen across the trail.

Doubletrack: A trail, jeep road, ATV route, or other track with two distinct ribbons of **tread,** typically with grass growing in between. No matter which side you choose, the other rut always looks smoother.

Endo: When the back wheel lifts off the ground, comes over your head, and sends you face-first into the ground. Try not to achieve this position, also known as a face plant.

Fall line: The angle and direction of a slope; the **line** you follow when gravity is in control and you aren't.

Get air: Jump, on purpose or not, and get both wheels off the ground. As in, "Way to get air, dude." (See also **bunny hop.**)

Graded: When a gravel road is scraped level to smooth out the washboards and potholes, it has been *graded*. In this book, a road is listed as graded only if it is regularly maintained. Not all such roads are graded every year, however.

Granny gear: The easiest gear on the bike; the innermost and smallest of the three front chainrings combined with the largest cog on the rear cluster. Shift down to your granny gear for the steepest climbs.

Hammer: To ride hard.

Hammerhead: Someone who goes out and **hammers**. In Durango, these people are generally known as racers.

Hondo or honch: See **hammerhead**.

Line: The route (or trajectory) between or over obstacles or through turns. **Tread** or trail refers to the ground you're riding on; the line is the path you choose within the tread (and exists mostly in the eye of the beholder).

Off the seat: Moving your butt behind the bike seat and over the rear tire; used for control on extremely steep descents. This position increases braking power, helps prevent **endos,** and reduces skidding.

Portage: To carry the bike, usually up a steep hill, across unrideable obstacles, or through a stream.

Quads: Thigh muscles (short for quadraceps); or maps in the USGS topographic series (short for quadrangles). Nice quads of either kind can help get you out of trouble in the backcountry.

Ratcheting: Also known as backpedaling; rotating the pedals backwards to avoid hitting them on rocks or other obstacles.

Sidehill: Where the trail crosses a slope. If the **tread** is narrow, keep your inside (uphill) pedal up to avoid hitting the ground. If the tread tilts downhill, you may have to use some body language to keep the bike plumb or vertical to avoid slipping out.

Singletrack: A trail, game run, or other track with only one ribbon of **tread.** But this is like defining an orgasm as a muscle cramp. Good singletrack is pure fun.

Spur: A side road or trail that splits off from the main route.

Surf: Riding through loose gravel or sand, when the wheels sway from side to side. Also *heavy surf:* frequent and difficult obstacles.

Suspension: A bike with front suspension has a shock-absorbing fork or stem. Rear suspension absorbs shock between the rear wheel and frame. A bike with both is said to be fully suspended.

Switchbacks: When a trail goes up a steep slope, it zig zags or *switchbacks* across the **fall line** to ease the gradient of the climb. Well-designed switchbacks make a turn with at least an 8-foot radius and remain fairly level within the turn itself. These are rare, however, and cyclists often struggle to ride through sharply angled, sloping switchbacks.

Track stand: Balancing on a bike in one place, without rolling forward appreciably. Control your side-to-side balance by applying pressure on the pedals and brakes and changing the angle of the front wheel, as needed. It takes practice but really comes in handy at stoplights, on **switchbacks,** and when trying to free a foot before falling.

Tread: The riding surface, particularly regarding **singletrack.**

Water bar: A log, rock, or other barrier placed in the **tread** to divert water off the trail and prevent erosion. Peeled logs can be slippery and cause bad falls, especially when they angle sharply across the trail or when wet.

About the Author

John Peel has been exploring Colorado via mountain bike since 1983. A native Coloradan, he has lived since 1990 in Durango, where he has worked at a bike shop, a mountaineering shop, and as sports editor for the local daily newspaper.